The Wayland Junior
ILLUSTRATED
ATLAS

WRITTEN BY
SHIRLEY WILLIS

ILLUSTRATED BY
NICK HEWETSON

CREATED AND DESIGNED BY
DAVID SALARIYA

HODDER
Wayland

an imprint of Hodder Children's Books

Contents

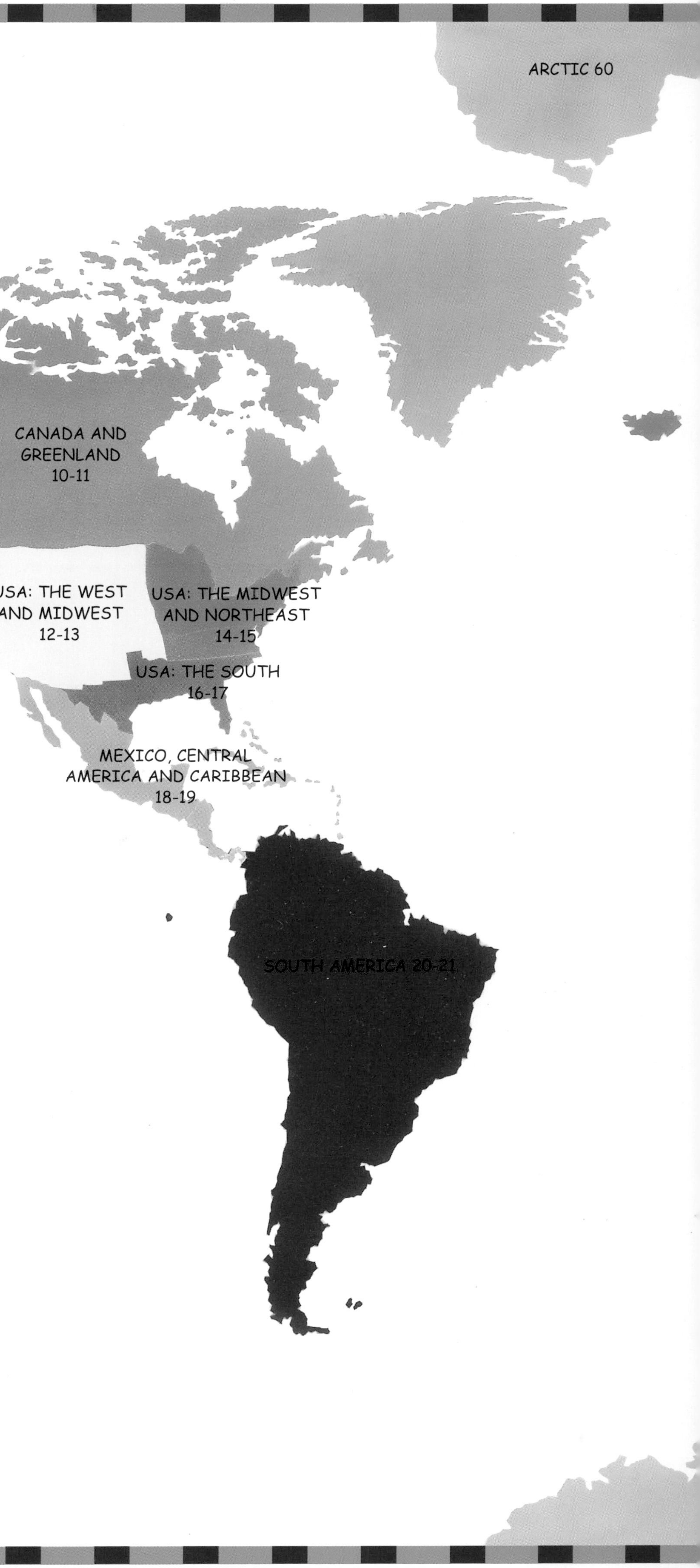

ARCTIC 60
CANADA AND GREENLAND 10-11
USA: THE WEST AND MIDWEST 12-13
USA: THE MIDWEST AND NORTHEAST 14-15
USA: THE SOUTH 16-17
MEXICO, CENTRAL AMERICA AND CARIBBEAN 18-19
SOUTH AMERICA 20-21

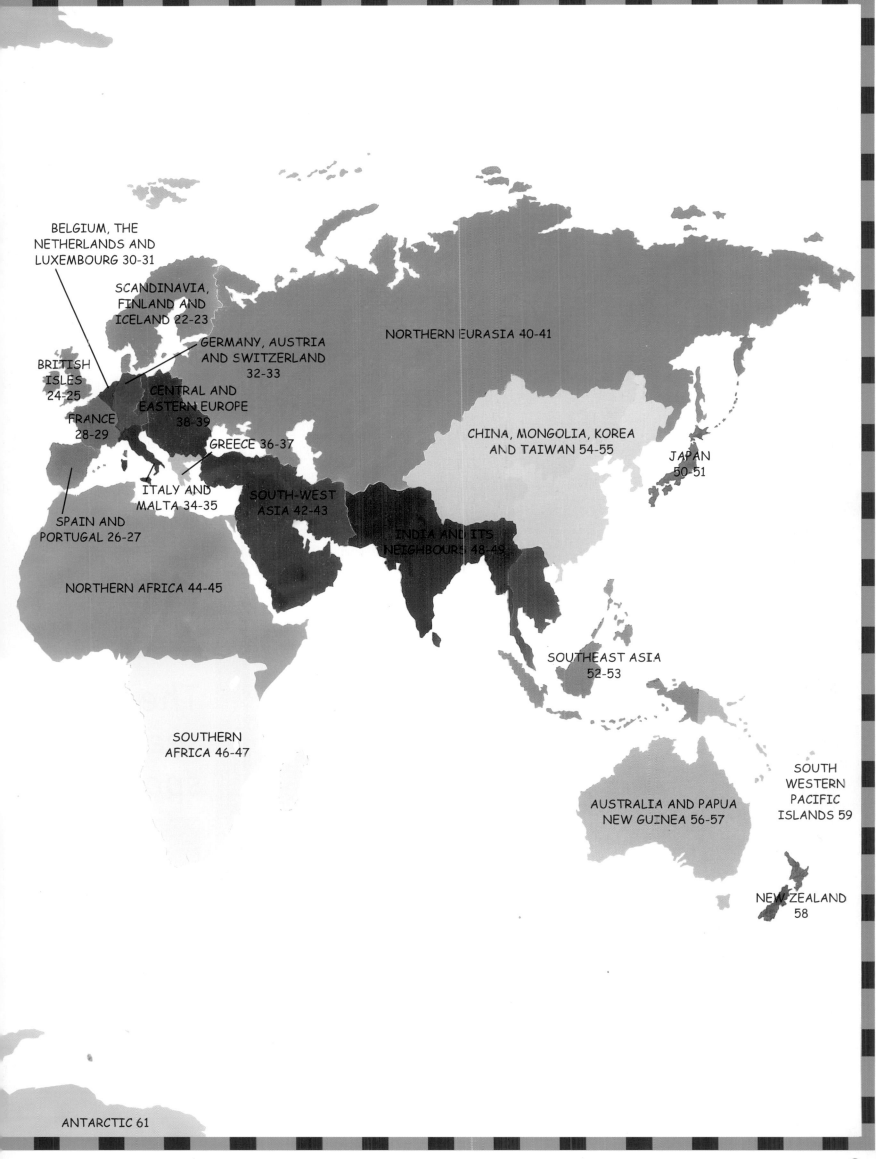

BELGIUM, THE NETHERLANDS AND LUXEMBOURG 30-31

SCANDINAVIA, FINLAND AND ICELAND 22-23

GERMANY, AUSTRIA AND SWITZERLAND 32-33

NORTHERN EURASIA 40-41

BRITISH ISLES 24-25

CENTRAL AND EASTERN EUROPE 38-39

CHINA, MONGOLIA, KOREA AND TAIWAN 54-55

JAPAN 50-51

FRANCE 28-29

GREECE 36-37

ITALY AND MALTA 34-35

SOUTH-WEST ASIA 42-43

INDIA AND ITS NEIGHBOURS 48-49

SPAIN AND PORTUGAL 26-27

NORTHERN AFRICA 44-45

SOUTHEAST ASIA 52-53

SOUTHERN AFRICA 46-47

SOUTH WESTERN PACIFIC ISLANDS 59

AUSTRALIA AND PAPUA NEW GUINEA 56-57

NEW ZEALAND 58

ANTARCTIC 61

3

The Earth in space

The Earth is a ball of rock that orbits the Sun. It depends on the Sun's energy for warmth and light.

The Earth is one of nine planets that orbit (circle) the Sun. Together they form the Solar System. Each planet orbits the Sun in an elliptical (oval) path. The length of a planet's orbit depends on its distance from the Sun. Mercury is closest and takes 88 days to orbit the Sun but Pluto takes 250 years because it is the outermost planet in our Solar System. The Earth's orbit takes about 365 days.

Uranus

Neptune

Saturn

Pluto

The Earth is always moving. As it orbits the Sun, the planet spins on its axis, making one complete turn every 24 hours. As one side of its surface is lit by the Sun, the other side is in darkness. This is why we have daytime and night-time.

The Earth's axis is an imaginary line running through its centre.

axis

The Earth seen from space.

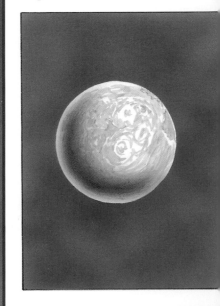

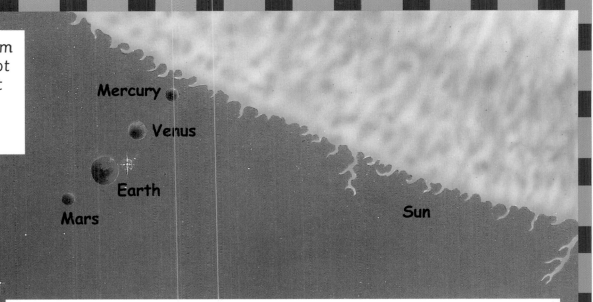

The Earth is 148,800,000 km from the Sun, making it neither too hot nor too cold. It is the only planet in the Solar System where life is known to exist.

Mercury

Venus

Earth

Mars

Sun

Jupiter

From space, the Earth is seen as a huge round ball. The planet looks blue because much of its surface is covered in oceans. Large land masses, called continents, can also be seen. Closer up, the Earth looks flat. From an aeroplane, the towns, roads, rivers and railtracks below divide the countryside into a huge patchwork pattern. People are too small to be seen from this distance. If you look down from a skyscraper, people below can be seen but look as small as ants. Cars on the streets look like children's toys.

The Earth seen from an aeroplane.

The Earth seen from a tall building.

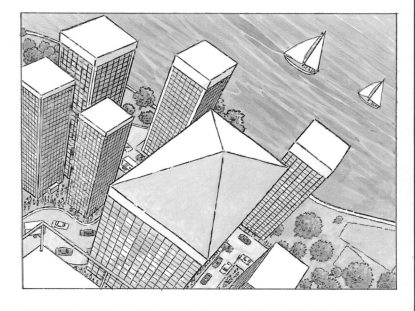

How the world becomes a flat map

A globe is a round map of the world. Map-makers make a flat map of the world for an atlas.

Our planet is made up of four layers (below). The surface of the Earth, on which we live, is called the crust. Every continent and ocean lies on the Earth's crust. Beneath the crust is a layer of rock called the mantle. Parts of the mantle are hot and molten (liquid) and can break through the crust to form a volcano. The core of the planet has two parts: the outer core is hot, molten metal and the inner core is solid metal.

Mantle (solid rock and liquid magma)

Inner core (solid metal)

Outer core (liquid)

Crust

Map-makers divide the world's surface into segments. These are laid side by side like the skin of an orange, but this leaves gaps in the map (above). Parts of the world are 'stretched' so that the map becomes whole. This process is called map projection. On the flat maps in an atlas the countries are shaped slightly differently than they are on a globe.

Map-makers use a grid of imaginary lines across the globe to help plot the exact positions of places. Lines of longitude are drawn from north to south and lines of latitude from east to west.

The equator is an imaginary line dividing the world in half. It is positioned at latitude 0° (zero degrees). The northern hemisphere is above it and the southern hemisphere below.

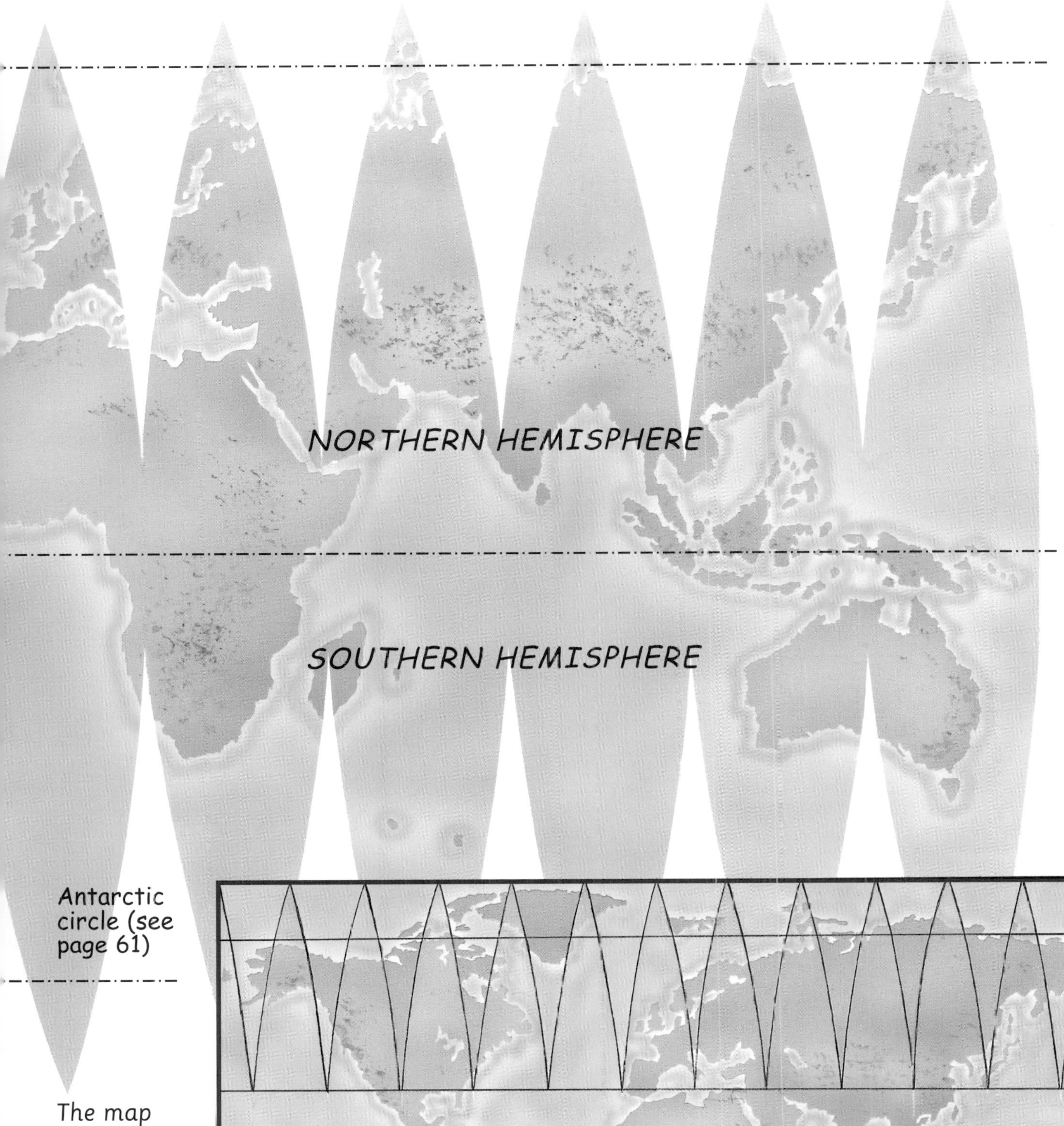

Arctic circle (see page 60)

NORTHERN HEMISPHERE

Equator

SOUTHERN HEMISPHERE

Antarctic circle (see page 61)

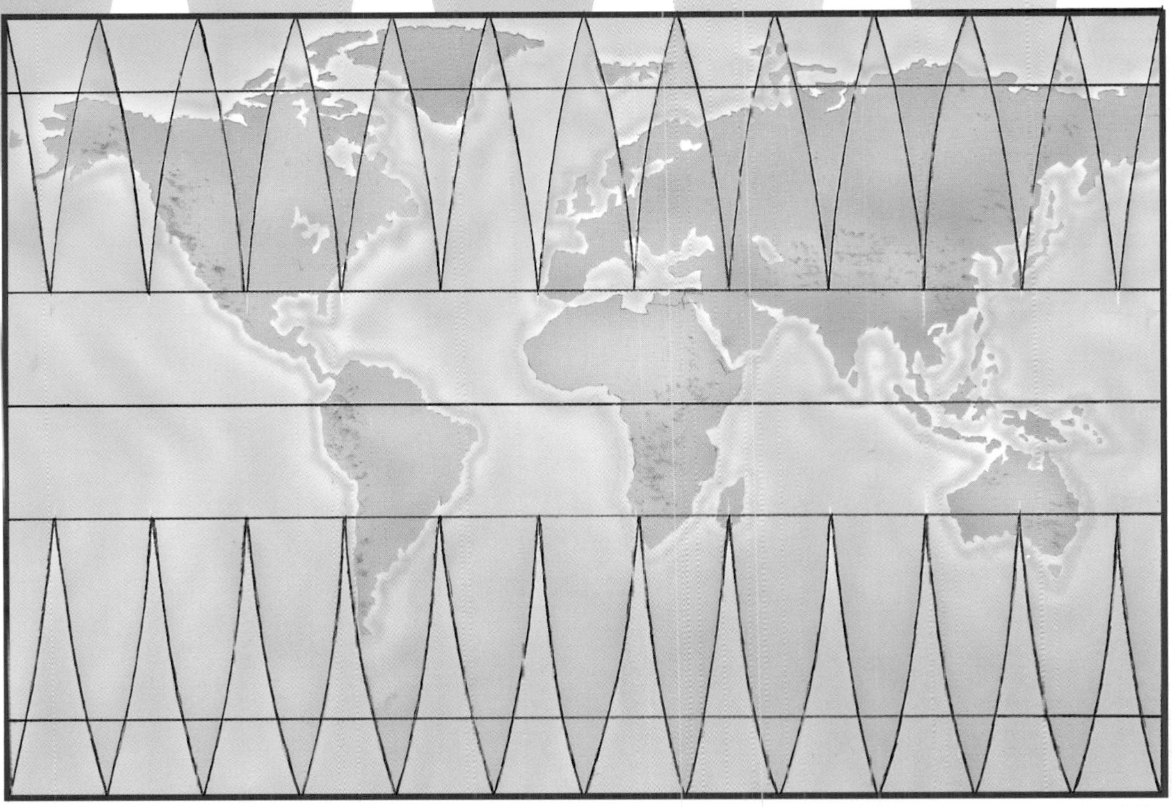

The map projections now fill the gaps between each segment (right). The countries have been stretched to complete the drawing of the flat map.

Arctic circle (66.5°N)

Equator (0°)

Antarctic circle (66.5°S)

How the pages work in this atlas

This is the kind of map you will find in this atlas. Each page shows a map of different countries of the world. The notes on this page explain the type of information given on each map.

Look on the map for buildings or other places of interest that are shown in the 'Can you find...' box.

A large, bold label in capital letters shows a country's name.

A thick dotted line shows the border between countries. A thin dotted line shows the border of states within a country.

The globe shows where the countries on each map are in the world.

A small label like this shows the name of a lake or river.

A curved label like this shows the name of the sea or ocean.

Go to the fact box for extra information about each country or continent.

Scandinavia, Fi and Iceland

Norway, Sweden and Denmark are known as Scandinavia. These countries are rich in natural resources: timber, fish, oil and natural gas. They have warm summers but bitterly cold winters.

Can you find...

a stave church?

Legoland?

NORWEGI
SEA

oil rig

stave church

skiing

S W
L. Stor

fishing boat

• Bergen

N O R W A Y

ski jumping

Norwe
spruce

Drottningholm
Palace

OSLO ■

SCANDINAVIA,
FINLAND AND
ICELAND

L. Vänern

L. Vättern

• Gothenburg

Little
Mermaid

Legoland

N O R T H

S E A

DENMARK

COPENHAGEN

Kalmar Castle

B A L T

GERMANY

Fact:

Hammerfest in Norway is the most northerly town in the world.

nd

Maps like this show a country and its position in relation to the region in the main map.

0 50 100 150 200 250 300 Miles
0 100 200 300 400 500 Kilometres
scale (Iceland)

Gullfoss Waterfall

puffins

ICELAND

REYKJAVIK

geysers

EUROPE

Each picture map has the wildlife, crops, buildings and places of interest shown where they can be found in each country.

ords are long sea inlets, nked by steep ountainsides. There are ndreds of them along Norwegian coast. mark and southern den have fertile land and Finland any lakes. The ic island of Iceland 000 km west of y.

iller whale

Hammerfest

reindeer

puffins

Sami people of Lapland

RUSSIA

hockey

elk

brown bear

wolf

A red spot shows an important town or city.

The pink areas are labelled showing the countries bordering the region.

EN

GULF OF BOTHNIA

L. Oulu

sauna

L. Pielinen

FINLAND

Ori

A red square shows the capital city of each country.

-breaker

Sannaa

0 50 100 150 200 250 Miles
0 100 200 300 400 Kilometres
scale

OLM

Turku

HELSINKI

E A

0 50 100 150 200 250 Miles
0 100 200 300 400 Kilometres
scale

Most of the maps cover two pages. This makes large countries and small countries look the same size. So, each map has its own scale to show the size of the region and distances between places. To compare the size of different countries see the world map on the contents page.

Read what the compass has to say about the region shown on the map.

N
W E
S

The Scandinavian people are descended from the Vikings.

N
W E
S

The compass points show N (North), S (South), E (East) and W (West). These directions help you to plot the position of places on the map. For example, Norway is west of Sweden.

Canada and Greenland

Canada is the second biggest country in the world but it does not have a large population. Few people live in northern Canada as the climate there is too harsh.

Canada has two official languages: English and French. Montreal (above), in Quebec is the largest French-speaking city in the world after Paris.

Can you find...

the C. N. Tower?

a research station?

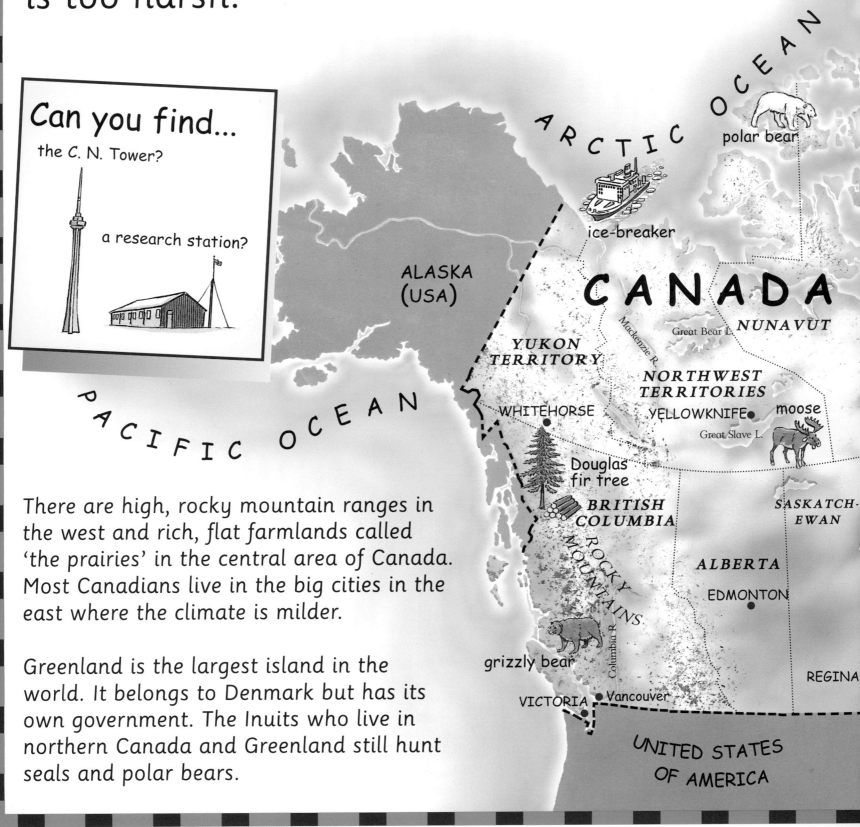

ARCTIC OCEAN

polar bear

ice-breaker

ALASKA (USA)

C A N A D A

NUNAVUT

Great Bear L.

Mackenzie R.

YUKON TERRITORY

NORTHWEST TERRITORIES

WHITEHORSE

YELLOWKNIFE

moose

Great Slave L.

PACIFIC OCEAN

Douglas fir tree

BRITISH COLUMBIA

SASKATCH-EWAN

ROCKY MOUNTAINS

ALBERTA

EDMONTON

grizzly bear

Columbia R.

REGINA

VICTORIA • Vancouver

UNITED STATES OF AMERICA

There are high, rocky mountain ranges in the west and rich, flat farmlands called 'the prairies' in the central area of Canada. Most Canadians live in the big cities in the east where the climate is milder.

Greenland is the largest island in the world. It belongs to Denmark but has its own government. The Inuits who live in northern Canada and Greenland still hunt seals and polar bears.

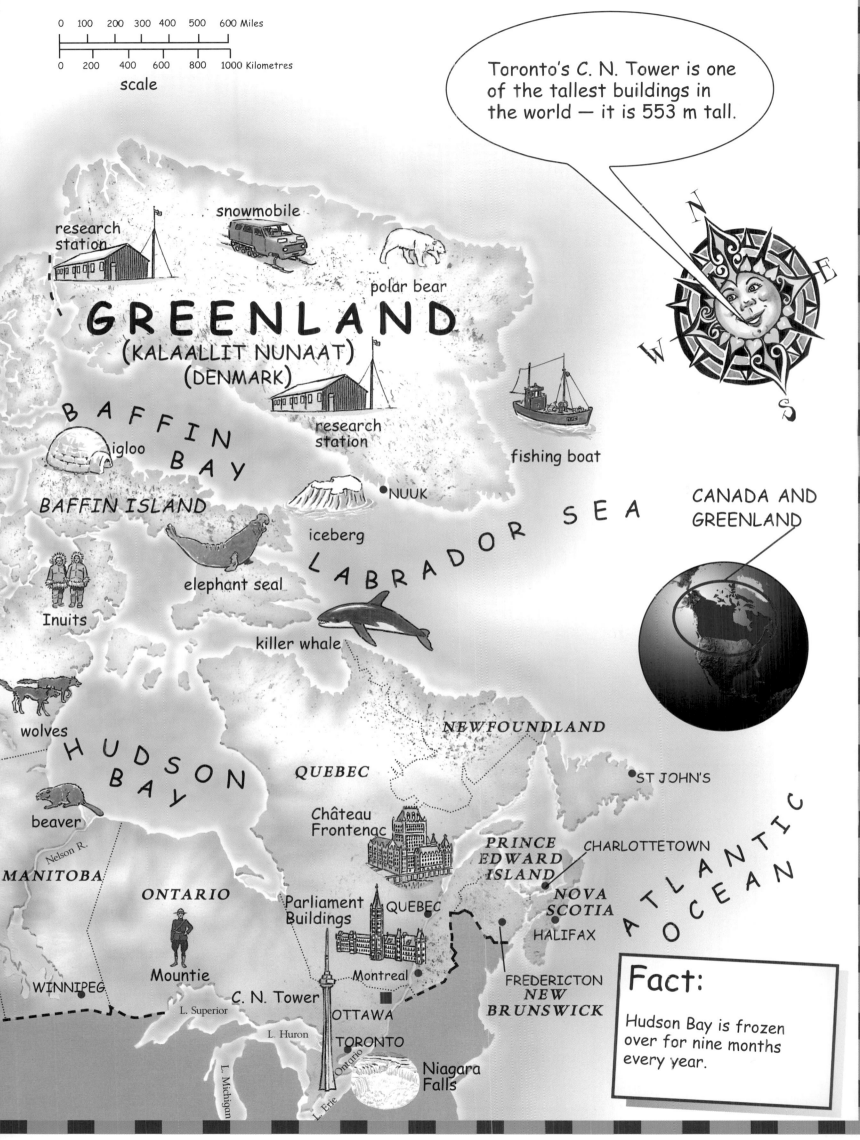

scale

0 100 200 300 400 500 600 Miles
0 200 400 600 800 1000 Kilometres

Toronto's C. N. Tower is one of the tallest buildings in the world — it is 553 m tall.

research station

snowmobile

polar bear

GREENLAND
(KALAALLIT NUNAAT)
(DENMARK)

BAFFIN BAY

igloo

BAFFIN ISLAND

research station

fishing boat

CANADA AND GREENLAND

iceberg

NUUK

LABRADOR SEA

elephant seal

Inuits

killer whale

wolves

HUDSON BAY

NEWFOUNDLAND

QUEBEC

ST JOHN'S

beaver

Nelson R.

Château Frontenac

PRINCE EDWARD ISLAND

CHARLOTTETOWN

MANITOBA

ONTARIO

Parliament Buildings

QUEBEC

NOVA SCOTIA

ATLANTIC OCEAN

Mountie

Montreal

HALIFAX

WINNIPEG

C. N. Tower

FREDERICTON
NEW BRUNSWICK

L. Superior

OTTAWA

L. Huron

TORONTO

L. Michigan

L. Erie

L. Ontario

Niagara Falls

Fact:

Hudson Bay is frozen over for nine months every year.

11

USA: The West and Midwest

The United States of America (USA) is one of the wealthiest countries in the world. It is made up of fifty states. The western states include Alaska in the far north and Hawaii, 4,000 km out in the Pacific Ocean.

The rugged landscape of the western states is dominated by the Rocky Mountains. California is the largest state in the region. More people live there than in any other American state.

scale

| 0 | 100 | 200 | 300 Miles |

| 0 | 100 | 200 | 300 | 400 | 500 Kilometres |

PACIFIC OCEAN

Seattle
OLYMPIA
WASHINGTON

Columbia R.

Portland
SALEM

OREGON

redwood tree

BOISE

Golden Gate Bridge

Reno
NEVADA
CARSON CITY
SACRAMENTO

San Francisco

wild horses

CALIFORNIA

grey whale

Las Vegas • L. Mead

HOLLYWOOD

Los Angeles

San Diego

Colorado R.

PACIFIC OCEAN

caribou
ALASKA

walrus

Anchorage

whale
JUNEAU

| 0 | 200 | 400 | 600 Miles |

| 0 | 200 | 400 | 600 | 800 | 1000 Kilometres |

scale (Alaska)

NORTH AMERICA

N
W   E
S

Hamburgers were invented in the USA and are now eaten all over the world.

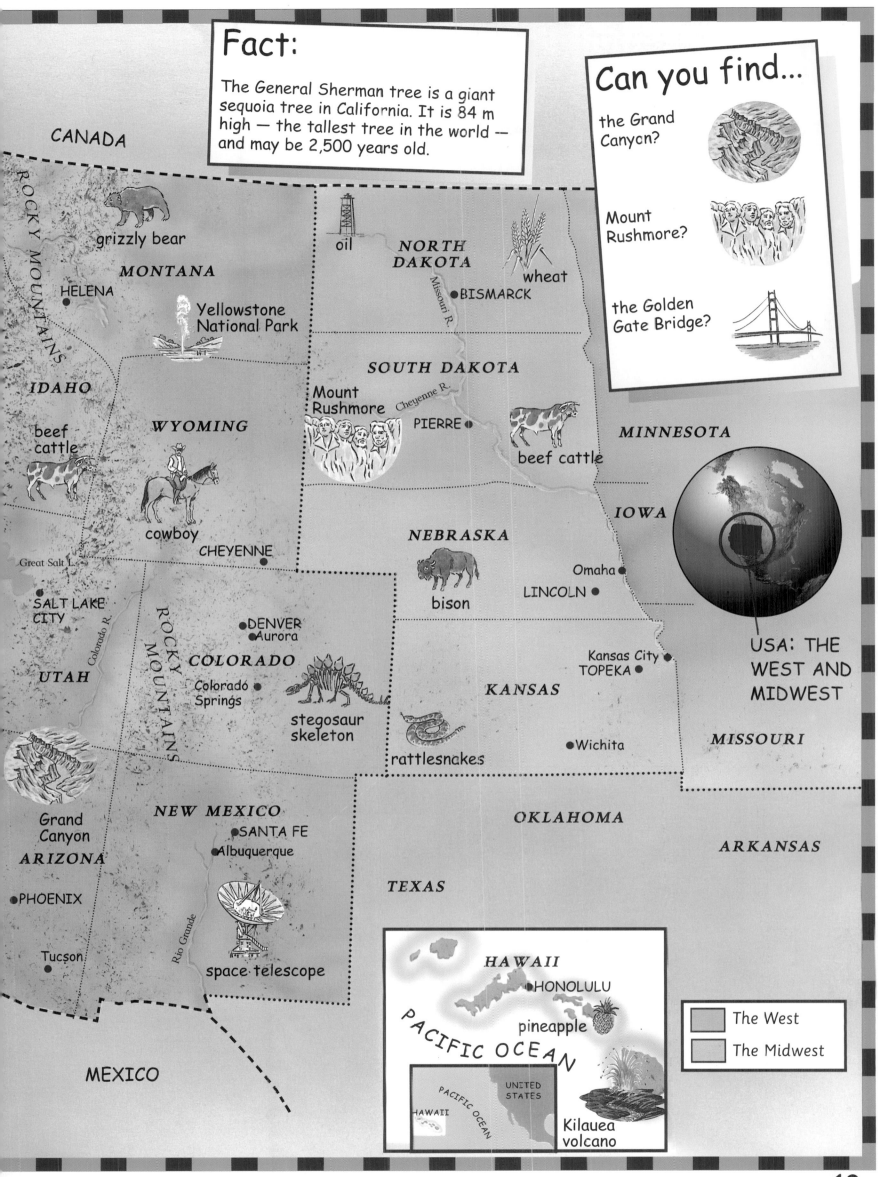

Fact:

The General Sherman tree is a giant sequoia tree in California. It is 84 m high — the tallest tree in the world — and may be 2,500 years old.

Can you find...

the Grand Canyon?

Mount Rushmore?

the Golden Gate Bridge?

CANADA

ROCKY MOUNTAINS

grizzly bear

MONTANA

HELENA

Yellowstone National Park

oil

NORTH DAKOTA

wheat

BISMARCK

Missouri R.

IDAHO

SOUTH DAKOTA

WYOMING

beef cattle

Mount Rushmore

Cheyenne R.

PIERRE

MINNESOTA

beef cattle

cowboy

CHEYENNE

Great Salt L.

SALT LAKE CITY

UTAH

Colorado R.

ROCKY MOUNTAINS

NEBRASKA

bison

IOWA

Omaha

LINCOLN

DENVER
Aurora

COLORADO

Colorado Springs

stegosaur skeleton

Kansas City
TOPEKA

KANSAS

rattlesnakes

Wichita

USA: THE WEST AND MIDWEST

MISSOURI

Grand Canyon

ARIZONA

PHOENIX

NEW MEXICO

SANTA FE

Albuquerque

OKLAHOMA

ARKANSAS

Tucson

Rio Grande

space telescope

TEXAS

HAWAII

HONOLULU

pineapple

PACIFIC OCEAN

PACIFIC OCEAN

HAWAII

UNITED STATES

Kilauea volcano

MEXICO

The West

The Midwest

13

USA: The Midwest and Northeast

The United States is the world's most industrial country. The area around the Great Lakes supplies most of the USA's iron and steel. Detroit is the centre of the American car industry.

USA: THE MIDWEST AND NORTHEAST

CANADA

L. Superior

bald eagle

moose

NORTH DAKOTA

black bear

MINNESOTA

maple tree

L. Huron

Minneapolis
ST PAUL

skunks

L. Ontario

WISCONSIN

Mississippi R.

L. Michigan

Niagara Falls

SOUTH DAKOTA

American football

MICHIGAN
LANSING

Milwaukee

Detroit

L. Erie

MADISON

IOWA

Chicago

car industry

cattle

Cedar Rapids

DES MOINES

Sears Tower

maize

baseball

Des Moines R.

NEBRASKA

Pittsburgh

ILLINOIS

INDIANA
INDIANAPOLIS

OHIO
COLUMBUS

wheat

SPRINGFIELD

Cincinnati

WEST VIRGINIA

MISSOURI

FRANKFORT

CHARLESTON

JEFFERSON CITY

St Louis

Ohio R.

Lexington

KANSAS

Wabash R.

KENTUCKY

Gateway Arch

Kentucky Derby

APPALACHIAN MOUNTAINS

Springfield

cotton

TENNESSEE

OKLAHOMA

ARKANSAS

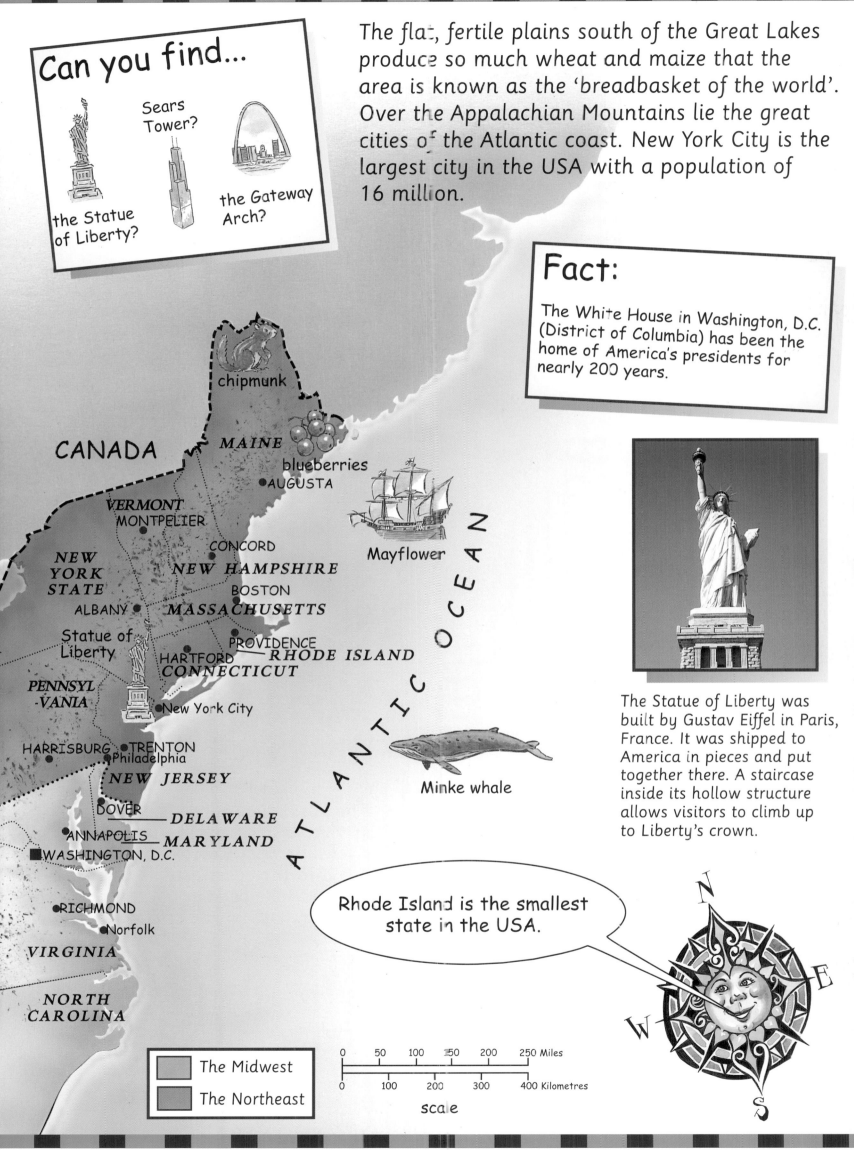

Can you find...

Sears Tower?

the Statue of Liberty?

the Gateway Arch?

The flat, fertile plains south of the Great Lakes produce so much wheat and maize that the area is known as the 'breadbasket of the world'. Over the Appalachian Mountains lie the great cities of the Atlantic coast. New York City is the largest city in the USA with a population of 16 million.

Fact:

The White House in Washington, D.C. (District of Columbia) has been the home of America's presidents for nearly 200 years.

CANADA

chipmunk

MAINE

blueberries

•AUGUSTA

VERMONT
MONTPELIER

•CONCORD

Mayflower

NEW YORK STATE

NEW HAMPSHIRE

ALBANY•

BOSTON•

MASSACHUSETTS

Statue of Liberty

•PROVIDENCE

RHODE ISLAND

HARTFORD•

CONNECTICUT

PENNSYL-VANIA

•New York City

HARRISBURG•

•TRENTON

•Philadelphia

NEW JERSEY

•DOVER

DELAWARE

•ANNAPOLIS

MARYLAND

■WASHINGTON, D.C.

•RICHMOND

•Norfolk

VIRGINIA

NORTH CAROLINA

ATLANTIC OCEAN

Minke whale

The Statue of Liberty was built by Gustav Eiffel in Paris, France. It was shipped to America in pieces and put together there. A staircase inside its hollow structure allows visitors to climb up to Liberty's crown.

Rhode Island is the smallest state in the USA.

The Midwest

The Northeast

0   50   100   150   200   250 Miles

0   100   200   300   400 Kilometres

scale

N
E
S
W

15

USA: The South

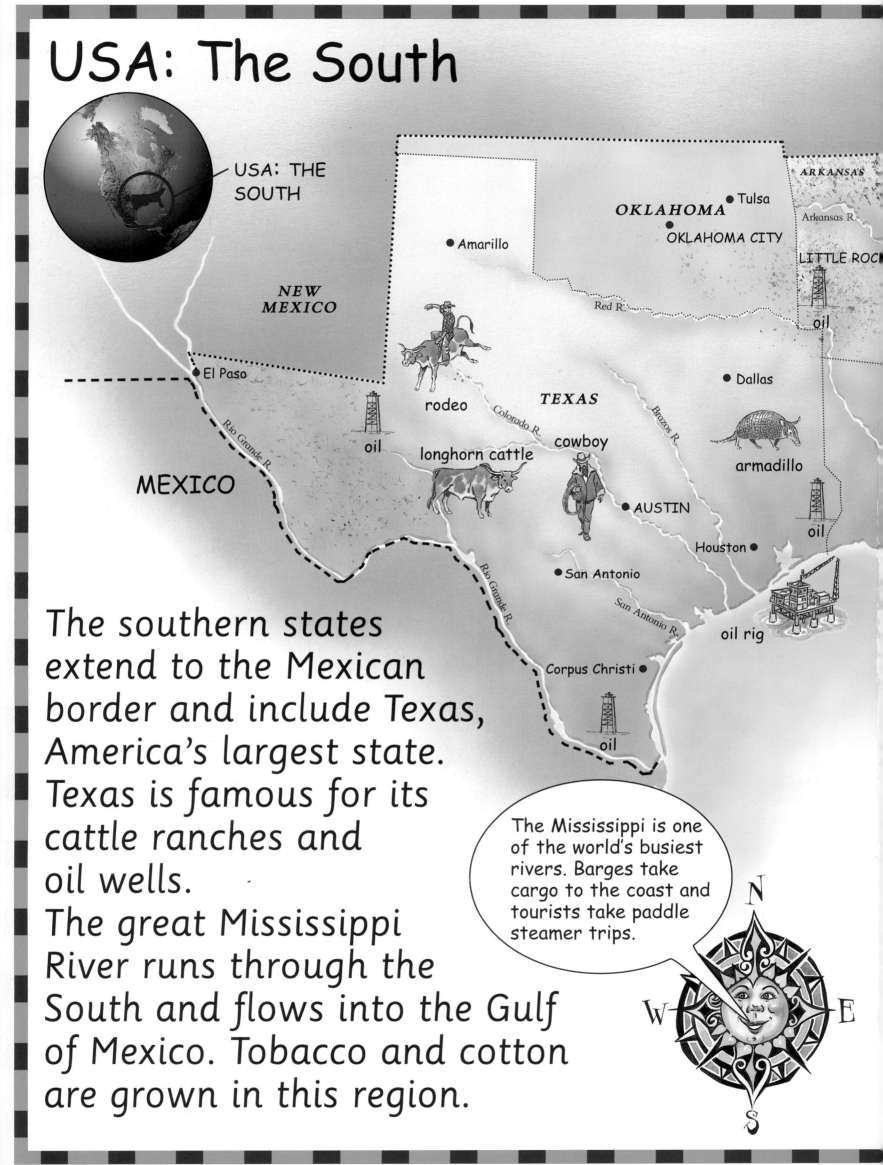

USA: THE SOUTH

ARKANSAS

OKLAHOMA

Tulsa

OKLAHOMA CITY

Arkansas R.

LITTLE ROCK

oil

Amarillo

NEW MEXICO

Red R.

rodeo

Colorado R.

TEXAS

Dallas

Brazos R.

armadillo

El Paso

oil

cowboy

Rio Grande R.

longhorn cattle

oil

MEXICO

AUSTIN

Houston

San Antonio

oil rig

Rio Grande R.

San Antonio R.

Corpus Christi

oil

The southern states extend to the Mexican border and include Texas, America's largest state. Texas is famous for its cattle ranches and oil wells.

The great Mississippi River runs through the South and flows into the Gulf of Mexico. Tobacco and cotton are grown in this region.

The Mississippi is one of the world's busiest rivers. Barges take cargo to the coast and tourists take paddle steamer trips.

N

W   E

S

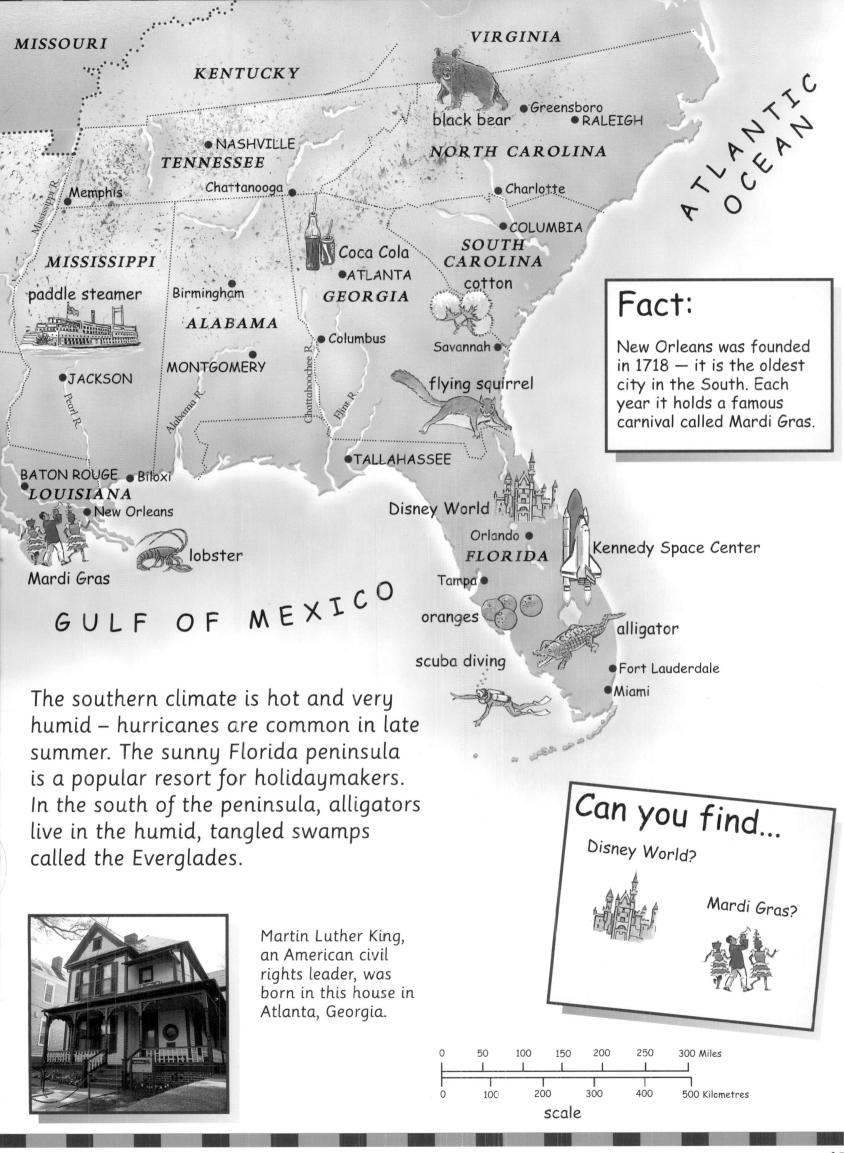

MISSOURI

KENTUCKY

VIRGINIA

black bear

• Greensboro
• RALEIGH

• NASHVILLE

TENNESSEE

NORTH CAROLINA

Memphis

Chattanooga

• Charlotte

Coca Cola

• COLUMBIA

MISSISSIPPI

SOUTH CAROLINA

paddle steamer

Birmingham

• ATLANTA

GEORGIA

cotton

ALABAMA

• Columbus

Savannah

• JACKSON

MONTGOMERY

flying squirrel

TALLAHASSEE

BATON ROUGE • Biloxi

LOUISIANA

• New Orleans

Disney World

Mardi Gras

lobster

Orlando •

FLORIDA

Kennedy Space Center

GULF OF MEXICO

Tampa •

oranges

alligator

scuba diving

• Fort Lauderdale
• Miami

ATLANTIC OCEAN

Fact:

New Orleans was founded in 1718 — it is the oldest city in the South. Each year it holds a famous carnival called Mardi Gras.

The southern climate is hot and very humid – hurricanes are common in late summer. The sunny Florida peninsula is a popular resort for holidaymakers. In the south of the peninsula, alligators live in the humid, tangled swamps called the Everglades.

Martin Luther King, an American civil rights leader, was born in this house in Atlanta, Georgia.

Can you find...

Disney World?

Mardi Gras?

| 0 | 50 | 100 | 150 | 200 | 250 | 300 Miles |

| 0 | 100 | 200 | 300 | 400 | 500 Kilometres |

scale

Mexico, Central America and the Caribbean

MEXICO, CENTRAL AMERICA AND THE CARIBBEAN

UNITED STATES OF AMERICA

seal

cactus

vampire bat

cotton

cotton

leatherback turtle

great white shark

MEXICO

PACIFIC OCEAN

GULF OF MEXICO

gold

maize

oil rig

National Cathedral

MEXICO CITY

Olmec stone heads

Acapulco

dolphin

Mexico and Central America link the continents of North and South America. The land is mountainous and much of it is covered by tropical rainforests. The Panama Canal, in the south of the region, provides a link for ships between the Atlantic and Pacific Oceans.

Can you find...

Chichén Itzá?

the Olmec stone heads?

the National Cathedral?

Mexico is this region's largest country. It is rich in silver and oil. Bananas and coffee grow in Central America and the Caribbean. The warm seas and climate of the Caribbean's volcanic islands attract many tourists.

This region is a hurricane zone. Fierce tropical storms sweep the Gulf of Mexico and the enormous waves they create cause a lot of damage.

CARIBBEAN ISLANDS

PUERTO RICO (US) SAN JUAN

BRITISH VIRGIN ISLANDS (UK)
ROAD TOWN
THE VALLEY

VIRGIN ISLANDS (US)

ANGUILLA (UK)

ANTIGUA AND BARBUDA

BASSETERRE

ST KITTS AND NEVIS

ST JOHNS

GUADELOUPE (FRANCE)

PLYMOUTH

BASSE-TERRE

MONTSERRAT (UK)

DOMINICA
ROSEAU

FORT-DE-FRANCE MARTINIQUE

CASTRIES ST LUCIA

ST VINCENT AND THE GRENADINES

BARBADOS

GRENADA
ST GEORGE'S

BRIDGETOWN

TRINIDAD AND TOBAGO
PORT OF SPAIN

CUBA

ATLANTIC OCEAN

SOUTH AMERICA

scale

0   100   200   300 Miles

0 100 200 300 400 500 Kilometres

NASSAU

BAHAMAS

scuba diving

tobacco

HAVANA

CUBA

DOMINICAN REPUBLIC

SANTO DOMINGO

PORT-AU-PRINCE

HAITI

cricket

JAMAICA

KINGSTON

C A R I B B E A N   S E A

Chichén Itzá

Cancún

oil rig

BELMOPAN

BELIZE

The city of Chichén Itzá was built in the 1100s by the people of the Maya civilisation.

GUATEMALA HONDURAS

GUATEMALA CITY

TEGUCIGALPA

SAN SALVADOR

EL SALVADOR

MANAGUA

ray

NICARAGUA

COSTA RICA

SAN JOSÉ

coffee

toucan

Panama Canal

PANAMA CITY

PANAMA

COLOMBIA

N

W   E

S

19

South America

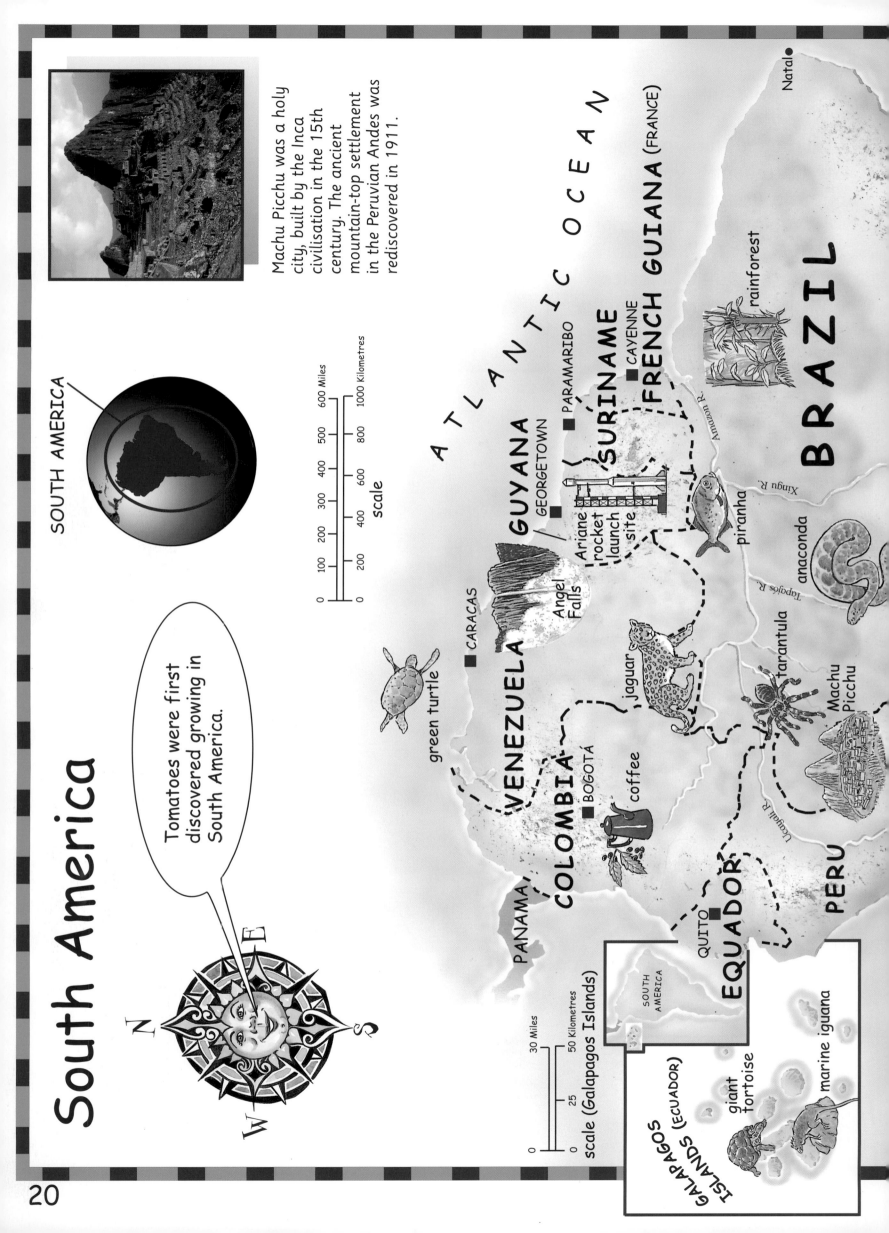

SOUTH AMERICA

Tomatoes were first discovered growing in South America.

Machu Picchu was a holy city, built by the Inca civilisation in the 15th century. The ancient mountain-top settlement in the Peruvian Andes was rediscovered in 1911.

scale

600 Miles
500
400
300
200
100
0

1000 Kilometres
800
600
400
200
0

ATLANTIC OCEAN

VENEZUELA
CARACAS
Angel Falls
green turtle

COLOMBIA
BOGOTÁ
coffee

PANAMA

GUYANA
GEORGETOWN
Ariane rocket launch site

SURINAME
PARAMARIBO

FRENCH GUIANA (FRANCE)
CAYENNE

Natal

BRAZIL
rainforest
Amazon R.
Xingu R.
piranha
Tapajos R.
anaconda

jaguar
tarantula
Machu Picchu

Ucayali R.

PERU

EQUADOR
QUITO
marine iguana

GALAPAGOS ISLANDS (ECUADOR)
giant tortoise

scale (Galapagos Islands)
30 Miles
25
0

50 Kilometres
25
0

SOUTH AMERICA

The Andes mountains run the length of the huge continent of South America. In the north, the Amazon River runs through vast tropical rainforests full of wildlife. In the south, millions of cattle and sheep are reared on fertile grasslands called the Pampas.

South America is rich in oil, silver, copper, coal and iron-ore. The continent's largest country, Brazil, is also the richest and most industrialised and is the world's leading coffee producer. Spanish is spoken throughout South America except in Brazil, where the language is Portuguese.

Map labels

Sugarloaf Mountain

Brasília Cathedral

BRASÍLIA

Statue of Christ

Rio de Janeiro

ATLANTIC OCEAN

diamond

PARAGUAY

ASUNCIÓN

BOLIVIA

LA PAZ

SUCRE

Andean condor

ANDES

llama

URUGUAY

MONTEVIDEO

BUENOS AIRES

ARGENTINA

SANTIAGO

volcano

CHILE

cattle

sheep

oil

oil

FALKLAND ISLANDS (UK)

STANLEY

LIMA

Fact:

Angel Falls in Venezuela is the highest waterfall in the world at over 800 m high.

Can you find...

the Statue of Christ?

Machu Picchu?

Angel Falls?

21

Scandinavia, Finland and Iceland

Norway, Sweden and Denmark are known as Scandinavia. These countries are rich in natural resources: timber, fish, oil and natural gas. They have warm summers but bitterly cold winters.

Fjords are long sea inlets, banked by steep mountainsides. There are hundreds of them along the Norwegian coast. Denmark and southern Sweden have fertile farmland and Finland has many lakes. The volcanic island of Iceland lies 1,000 km west of Norway.

scale (Iceland)

0   50 100 150 200 250 300 Miles
0   100   200   300   400   500 Kilometres

Gullfoss Waterfall

puffins

ICELAND

REYKJAVIK

geysers

EUROPE

RUSSIA

wolf

Sami people of Lapland

brown bear

reindeer

Hammerfest

elk

ice hockey

killer whale

puffins

N O R W E G I A N   S E A

Can you find...

Legoland?

a stave church?

22

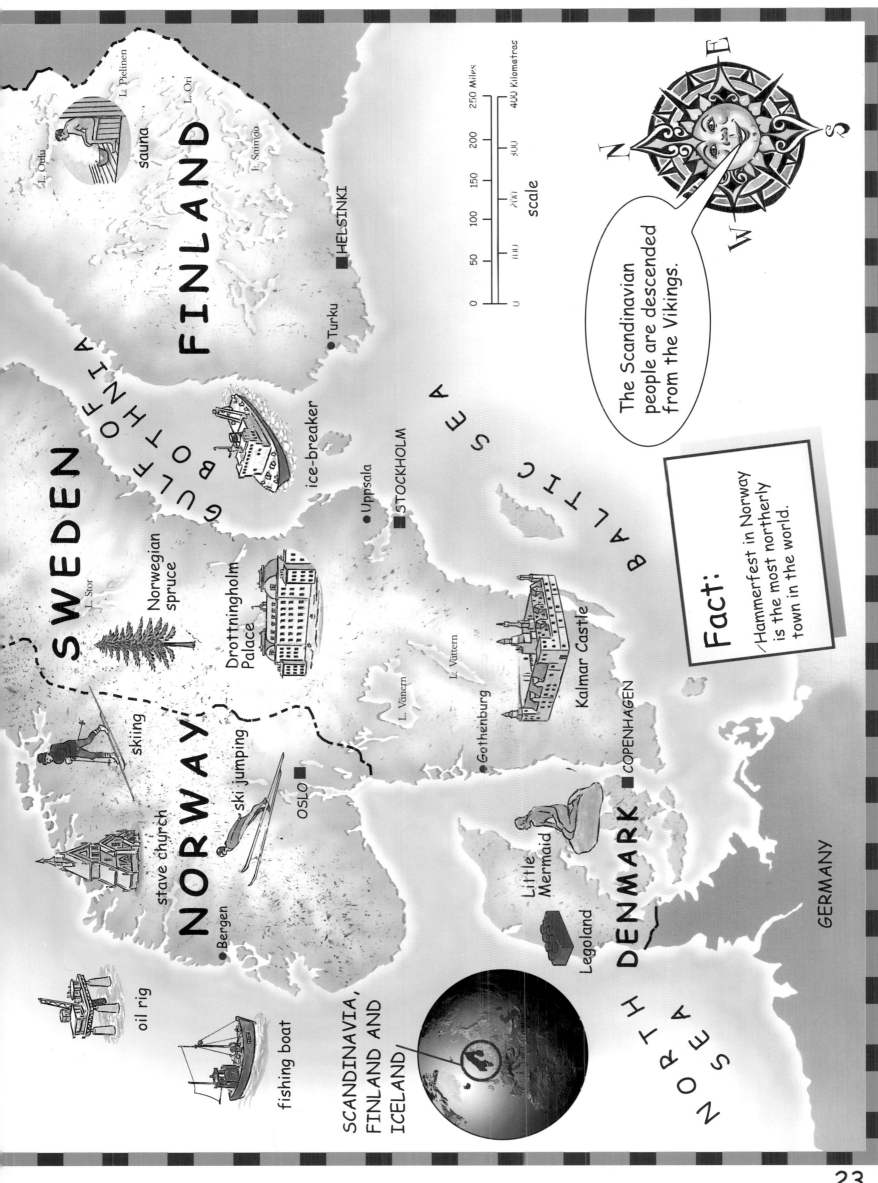

FINLAND

sauna

L. Ortu
L. Pielinen
L. Ori
L. Saimaa

HELSINKI

Turku

SWEDEN

GULF OF BOTHNIA

ice-breaker

Norwegian spruce

L. Stor

Drottningholm Palace

Uppsala

STOCKHOLM

BALTIC SEA

L. Vänern

L. Vättern

Kalmar Castle

Gothenburg

skiing

NORWAY

ski jumping

stave church

OSLO

Bergen

oil rig

fishing boat

Little Mermaid

Legoland

DENMARK

COPENHAGEN

GERMANY

NORTH SEA

SCANDINAVIA, FINLAND AND ICELAND

The Scandinavian people are descended from the Vikings.

scale

0   50   100 150 200 250 Miles
0   100 200 300 400 Kilometres

N
E
S
W

Fact:

Hammerfest in Norway is the most northerly town in the world.

23

The British Isles

The United Kingdom (UK) and Ireland are known as the British Isles. Much of the land is farmed, but there are many large cities. London, the biggest city and the capital of the UK, is a major financial and cultural centre. The Channel Tunnel links the UK with mainland Europe.

Fact:

The Forth rail-bridge, Scotland, was the first major bridge in the world to be built of steel.

THE BRITISH ISLES

SHETLAND ISLES (UK)

Lerwick

UK

60 Miles

100 Kilometres

75

50

30

25

0   0

scale (Shetland Isles)

150 Miles

200 Kilometres

100

100

50

0   0

scale

Can you find...

the Giant's Causeway?

Edinburgh Castle?

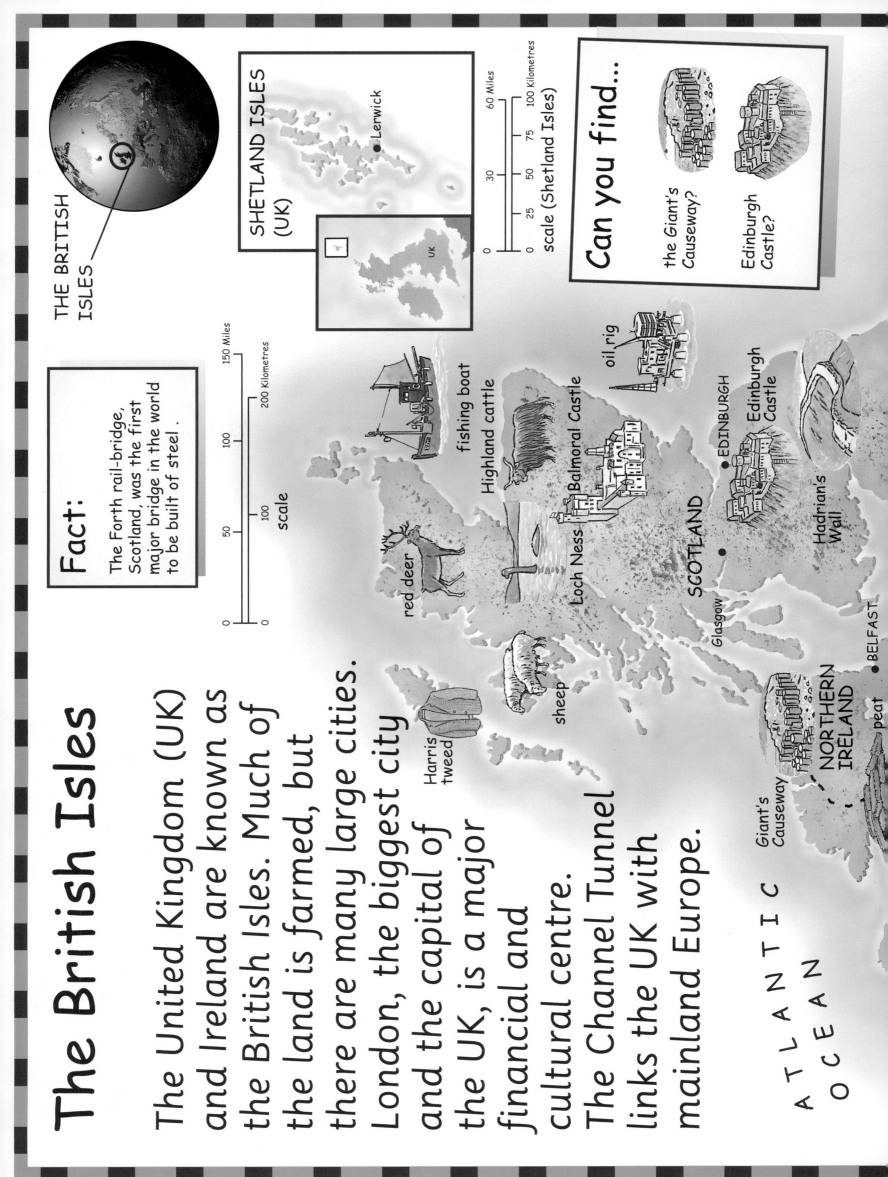

oil rig

fishing boat

Highland cattle

Balmoral Castle

red deer

Loch Ness

sheep

Harris tweed

EDINBURGH

Edinburgh Castle

SCOTLAND

Glasgow

Hadrian's Wall

BELFAST

NORTHERN IRELAND

Giant's Causeway

peat

ATLANTIC OCEAN

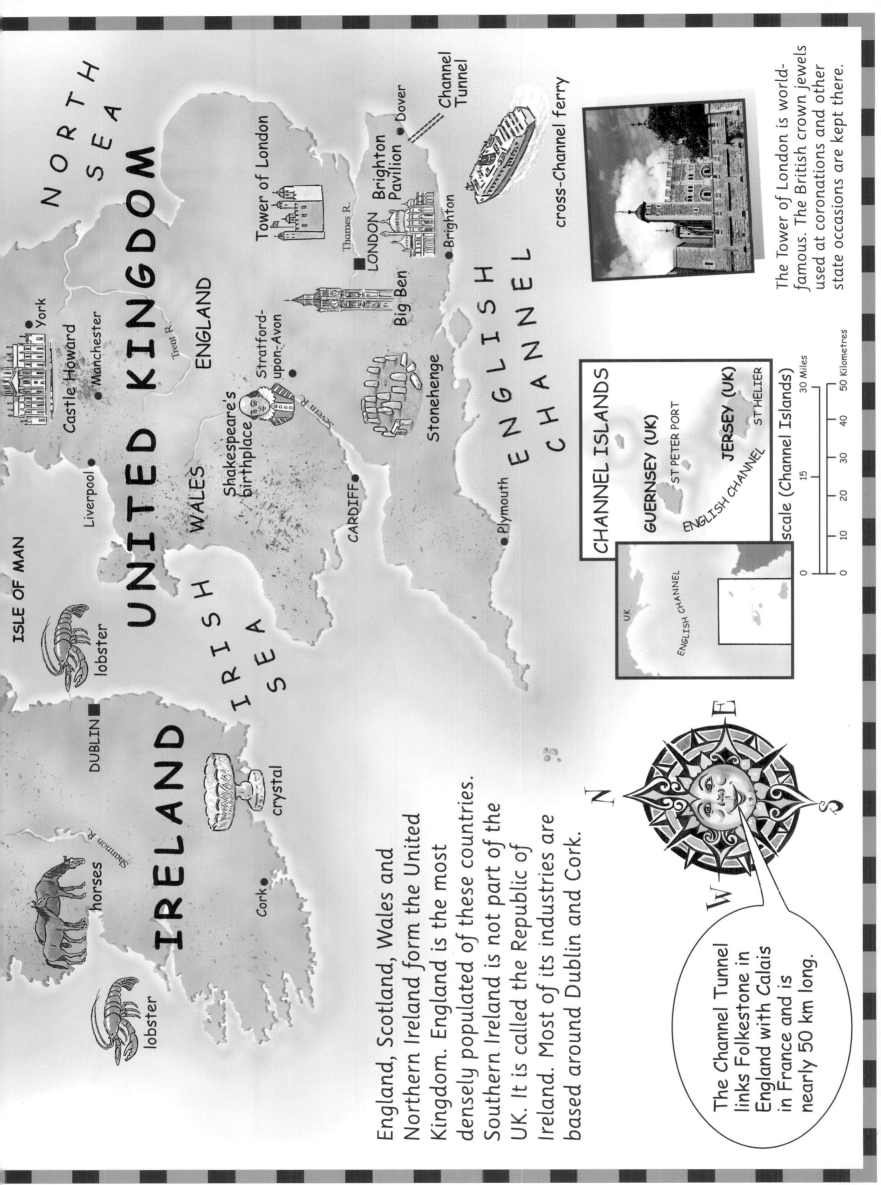

NORTH SEA

UNITED KINGDOM

ISLE OF MAN

IRISH SEA

York

Castle Howard

Manchester

Liverpool

lobster

Trent R.

ENGLAND

WALES

Shakespeare's birthplace

Stratford-upon-Avon

Severn R.

CARDIFF

Stonehenge

Tower of London

Thames R.

LONDON

Big Ben

Brighton Pavilion

Brighton

Dover

Channel Tunnel

Plymouth

ENGLISH CHANNEL

cross-Channel ferry

The Tower of London is world-famous. The British crown jewels used at coronations and other state occasions are kept there.

CHANNEL ISLANDS

GUERNSEY (UK)

ST PETER PORT

JERSEY (UK)

ST HELIER

ENGLISH CHANNEL

scale (Channel Islands)

30 Miles

15

0

50 Kilometres

40

30

20

10

0

UK

ENGLISH CHANNEL

IRELAND

DUBLIN

Shannon R.

horses

Cork

crystal

lobster

England, Scotland, Wales and Northern Ireland form the United Kingdom. England is the most densely populated of these countries. Southern Ireland is not part of the UK. It is called the Republic of Ireland. Most of its industries are based around Dublin and Cork.

N E W S

The Channel Tunnel links Folkestone in England with Calais in France and is nearly 50 km long.

25

Spain and Portugal

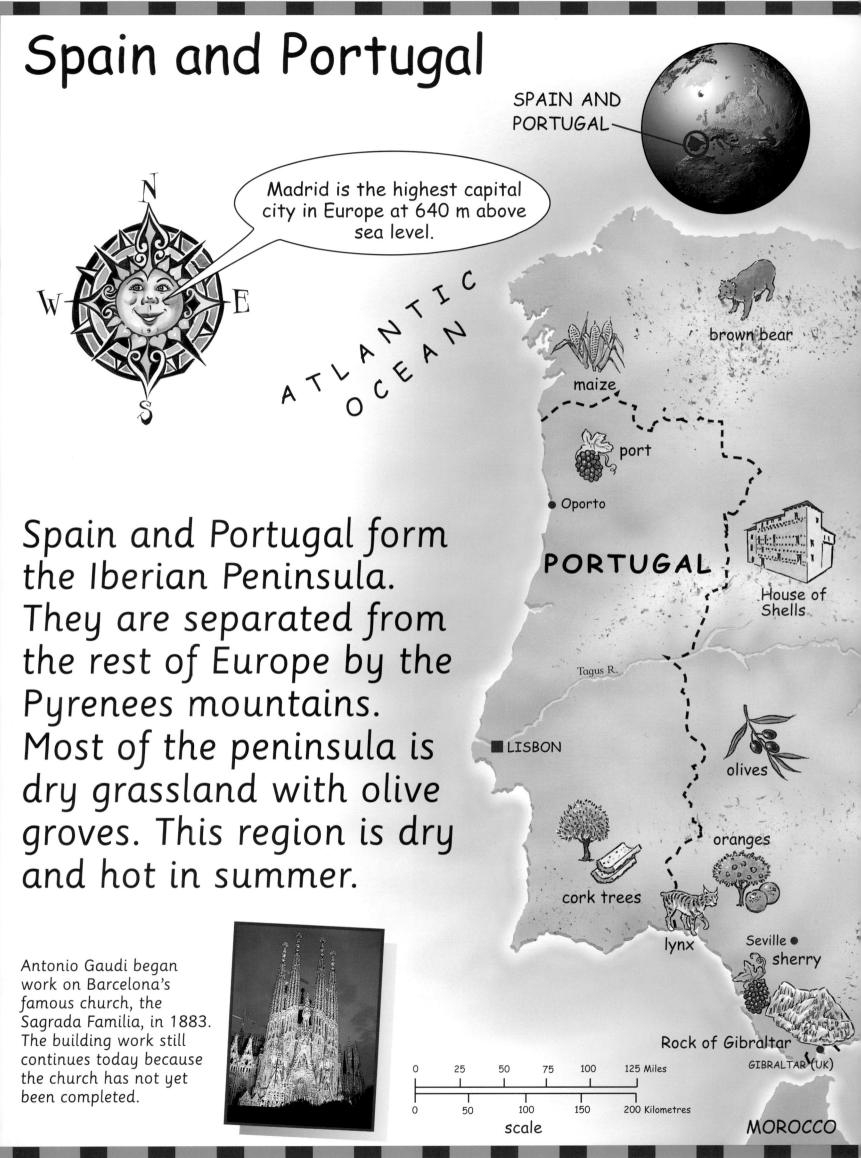

SPAIN AND PORTUGAL

Madrid is the highest capital city in Europe at 640 m above sea level.

N
W   E
S

ATLANTIC OCEAN

brown bear

maize

port

• Oporto

PORTUGAL

House of Shells

Tagus R.

■ LISBON

olives

oranges

cork trees

lynx

Seville •
sherry

Rock of Gibraltar
GIBRALTAR (UK)

Spain and Portugal form the Iberian Peninsula. They are separated from the rest of Europe by the Pyrenees mountains. Most of the peninsula is dry grassland with olive groves. This region is dry and hot in summer.

Antonio Gaudi began work on Barcelona's famous church, the Sagrada Familia, in 1883. The building work still continues today because the church has not yet been completed.

0   25   50   75   100   125 Miles

0   50   100   150   200 Kilometres

scale

MOROCCO

26

Fact:

Europe's only desert is near Almeria on the south coast of Spain. Less than 170 mm of rain falls there each year.

Can you find...

the Sagrada Familia?

Alhambra Palace?

BAY OF BISCAY

FRANCE

•Bilbao

cave paintings (Altamira)

running with the bulls

PYRENEES

skiing

wild boar

Sagrada Familia

SPAIN

Ebro R.

•Barcelona

wine

bullfighting

olives

oil rig

■ MADRID

oranges

BALEARIC ISLANDS (SPAIN)

MINORCA

•Mahón

MAJORCA

•Palma

•Toledo

•Valencia

windmill

sunflowers

almonds

IBIZA

fishing boat

flamenco dancers

Alhambra Palace   •Almeria

sardines

tuna

Most Spanish people live in towns and cities but many make their living from farming or fishing. Tourism is a major industry in Spain and Portugal and both countries attract holidaymakers all year round. Orange groves and cork trees flourish in the south – most of the world's supply of cork is produced by Spain and Portugal.

MEDITERRANEAN SEA

France

France is one of Europe's largest farming and industrial countries. Its mild climate becomes hotter and drier towards its southern borders with Italy and Spain. France is famous for its fine food and wines.

FRANCE

ENGLISH CHANNEL

Le Havre

Mont St. Michel

Bayeux Tapestry

Standing Stones (Carnac)

Loire R.

Nantes

Can you find...

the Eiffel Tower?

Mont St. Michel?

the amphitheatre at Arles?

BAY OF BISCAY

brandy

Lascaux cave paintings

Bordeaux

Garonne R.

wine

brown bear

SPAIN

Much of France is farmland but most people now live in towns and cities.

The area around Paris, the capital city, is densely populated. Paris is famous for its great fashion houses, its smart restaurants and as a centre for the arts.

Andorra and Monaco are small, independent countries. Many wealthy people choose to live in Monaco because of its tax laws.

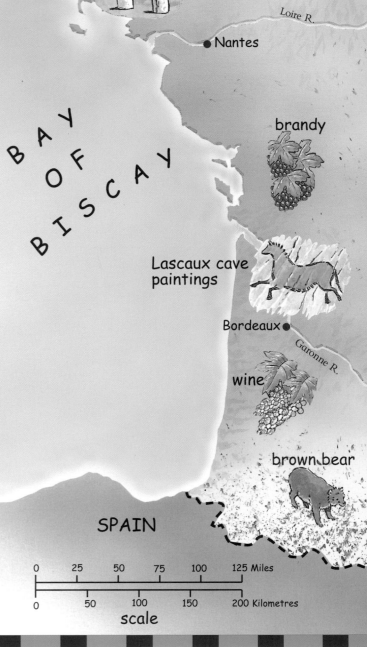

0	25	50	75	100	125 Miles
0		50	100	150	200 Kilometres

scale

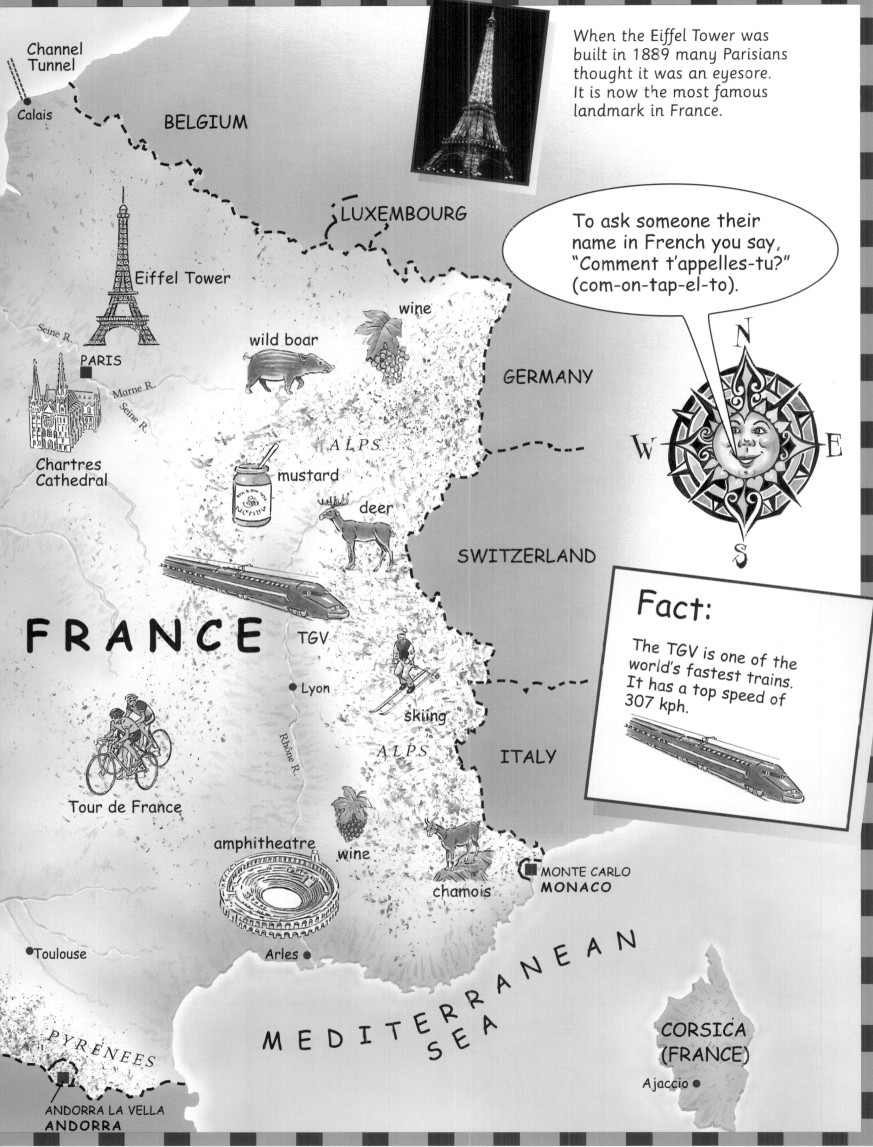

Channel Tunnel

Calais

BELGIUM

When the Eiffel Tower was built in 1889 many Parisians thought it was an eyesore. It is now the most famous landmark in France.

LUXEMBOURG

Eiffel Tower

Seine R.

PARIS

Marne R.

Seine R.

Chartres Cathedral

wine

wild boar

GERMANY

To ask someone their name in French you say, "Comment t'appelles-tu?" (com-on-tap-el-to).

ALPS

mustard

deer

SWITZERLAND

N

W E

S

Fact:

The TGV is one of the world's fastest trains. It has a top speed of 307 kph.

FRANCE

TGV

Lyon

skiing

Rhône R.

ALPS

ITALY

Tour de France

amphitheatre

wine

chamois

MONTE CARLO
MONACO

Toulouse

Arles

MEDITERRANEAN SEA

CORSICA (FRANCE)

Ajaccio

PYRENEES

ANDORRA LA VELLA
ANDORRA

Belgium, the Netherlands and Luxembourg

This part of Europe is called 'the Low Countries'. Most of the land in these countries is flat. Large areas of land have been reclaimed from the sea by draining it and building long dykes (walls) to protect the land from flooding.

Belgium is famous for lacemaking and fine chocolate.

BELGIUM, THE NETHERLANDS AND LUXEMBOURG

windmill

clogs

seal

ice skating

THE NETHERLANDS

GERMANY

canal house

AMSTERDAM

Ijssel R.

Delft pottery

Edam cheese

diamond cutting

tulips

The Hague

Rotterdam

Lek R.

Waal R.

NORTH SEA

N E S W

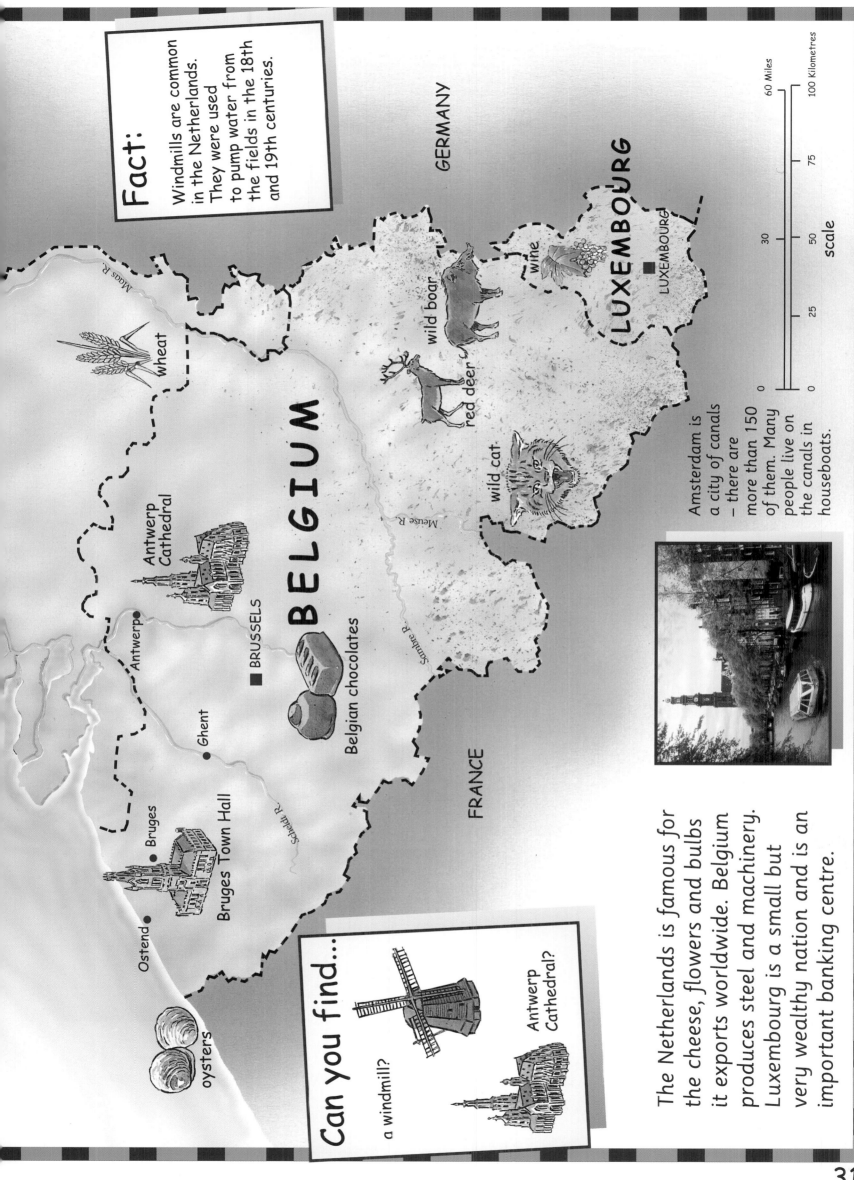

Fact:

Windmills are common in the Netherlands. They were used to pump water from the fields in the 18th and 19th centuries.

GERMANY

LUXEMBOURG

60 Miles

100 Kilometres

0   25   50   75   100

0   30   60   90   scale

Maas R.

wheat

wild boar

red deer

wine

LUXEMBOURG
◼ LUXEMBOURG

BELGIUM

Antwerp Cathedral

Meuse R.

wild cat

Antwerp●
Antwerp

◼ BRUSSELS

Belgian chocolates

Ghent

Sambre R.

FRANCE

Schelde R.

Bruges Town Hall

● Bruges

Ostend ●

oysters

Amsterdam is a city of canals – there are more than 150 of them. Many people live on the canals in houseboats.

Can you find...

a windmill?

Antwerp Cathedral?

The Netherlands is famous for the cheese, flowers and bulbs it exports worldwide. Belgium produces steel and machinery. Luxembourg is a small but very wealthy nation and is an important banking centre.

Neuschwanstein Castle was built by King Louis II. Walt Disney based his fairy-tale castle on this fantastic building.

Germany, Austria and Switzerland

Germany is a wealthy industrial nation. It produces cars, electrical goods, wines and beers. It has a large population and many large cities. There are forests, long rivers and lots of fine castles. Germany's large rivers are important for transporting goods around the country.

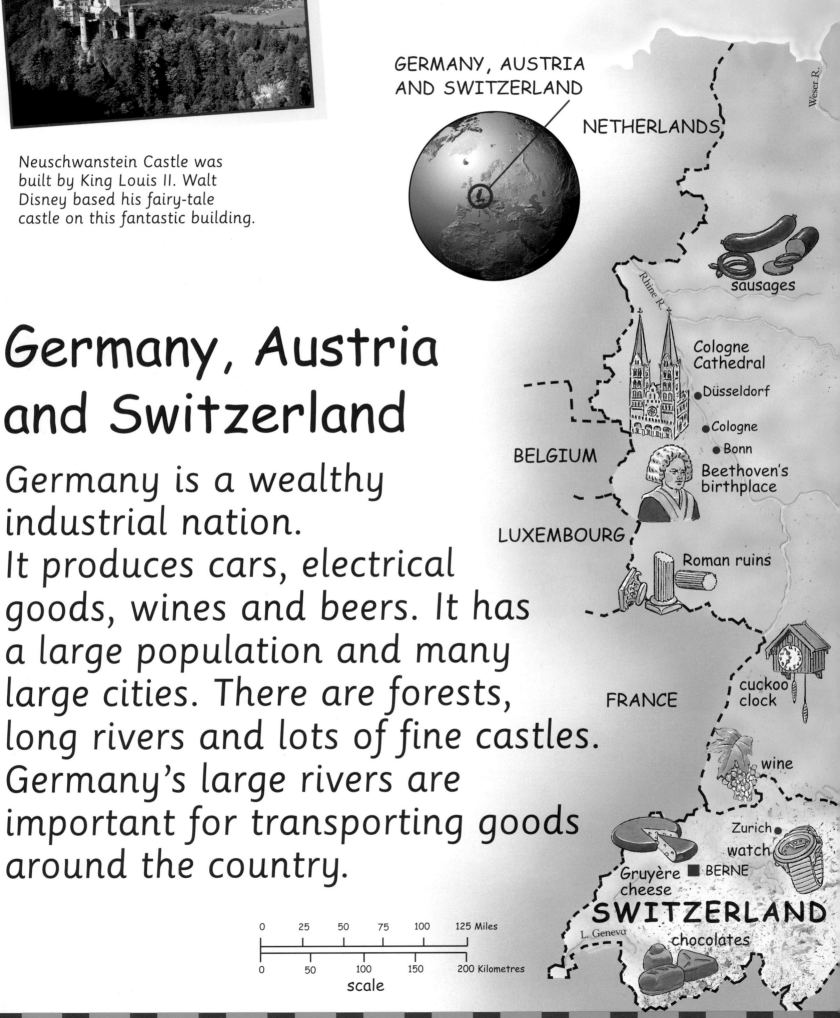

GERMANY, AUSTRIA AND SWITZERLAND

NORTH SEA

NETHERLANDS

Weser R.

sausages

Rhine R.

Cologne Cathedral

Düsseldorf

Cologne

Bonn

Beethoven's birthplace

BELGIUM

LUXEMBOURG

Roman ruins

FRANCE

cuckoo clock

wine

Zurich

watch

Gruyère cheese

BERNE

SWITZERLAND

L. Geneva

chocolates

scale

0	25	50	75	100	125 Miles
0	50	100	150	200 Kilometres	

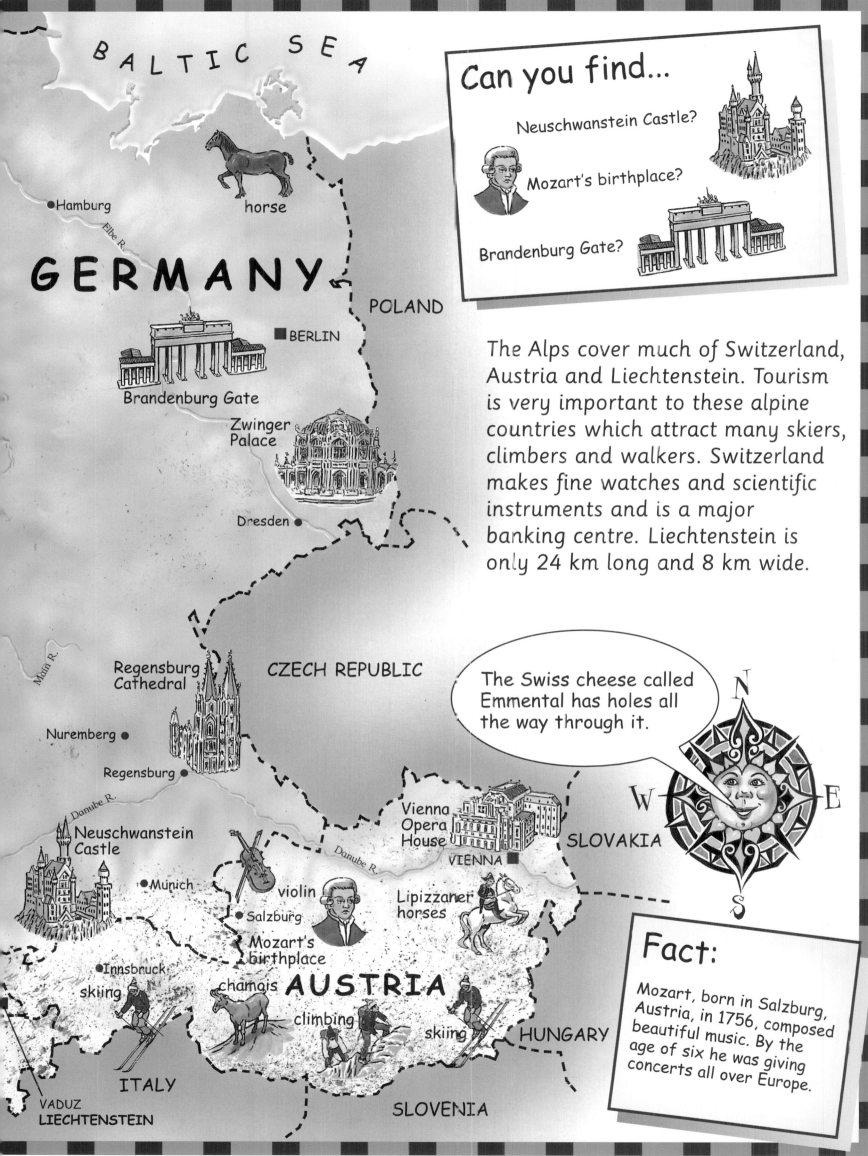

BALTIC SEA

•Hamburg

horse

Elbe R.

GERMANY

Brandenburg Gate

POLAND

■ BERLIN

Zwinger Palace

Dresden •

Main R.

Regensburg Cathedral

CZECH REPUBLIC

Nuremberg •

Regensburg •

Danube R.

Neuschwanstein Castle

•Munich

violin

Salzburg

Mozart's birthplace

•Innsbruck

chamois AUSTRIA

skiing

climbing

Vienna Opera House

Danube R.

VIENNA ■

Lipizzaner horses

SLOVAKIA

skiing

HUNGARY

ITALY

VADUZ
LIECHTENSTEIN

SLOVENIA

Can you find...

Neuschwanstein Castle?

Mozart's birthplace?

Brandenburg Gate?

The Alps cover much of Switzerland, Austria and Liechtenstein. Tourism is very important to these alpine countries which attract many skiers, climbers and walkers. Switzerland makes fine watches and scientific instruments and is a major banking centre. Liechtenstein is only 24 km long and 8 km wide.

The Swiss cheese called Emmental has holes all the way through it.

N
W   E
S

Fact:

Mozart, born in Salzburg, Austria, in 1756, composed beautiful music. By the age of six he was giving concerts all over Europe.

Italy and Malta

Italy is famous for its art, food, fashion and cars. Most of its population, industry and farmland are concentrated along the River Po in the north.

Can you find...

Pompeii?   the Leaning Tower of Pisa?   the Colosseum?

Fact:

Pizza is a traditional food that was invented in Italy. It is now eaten worldwide.

ADRIATIC SEA

SLOVENIA

CROATIA

AUSTRIA

ALPS

SWITZERLAND

ALPS

St. Marks Square

Venice

L. Garda

violin

Milan Cathedral

Milan

Po R.

Parmesan cheese

Turin

wine

olives

FRANCE

gondolier

pasta

Parma ham

Leaning Tower of Pisa

Pisa

Florence Cathedral

Florence

SAN MARINO
SAN MARINO

Tiber R.

ITALY

Colosseum

ROME
VATICAN CITY

Vatican

LIGURIAN SEA

CORSICA (FRANCE)

scale

0   25   50   75   100   125 Miles

0   50   100   150   200 Kilometres

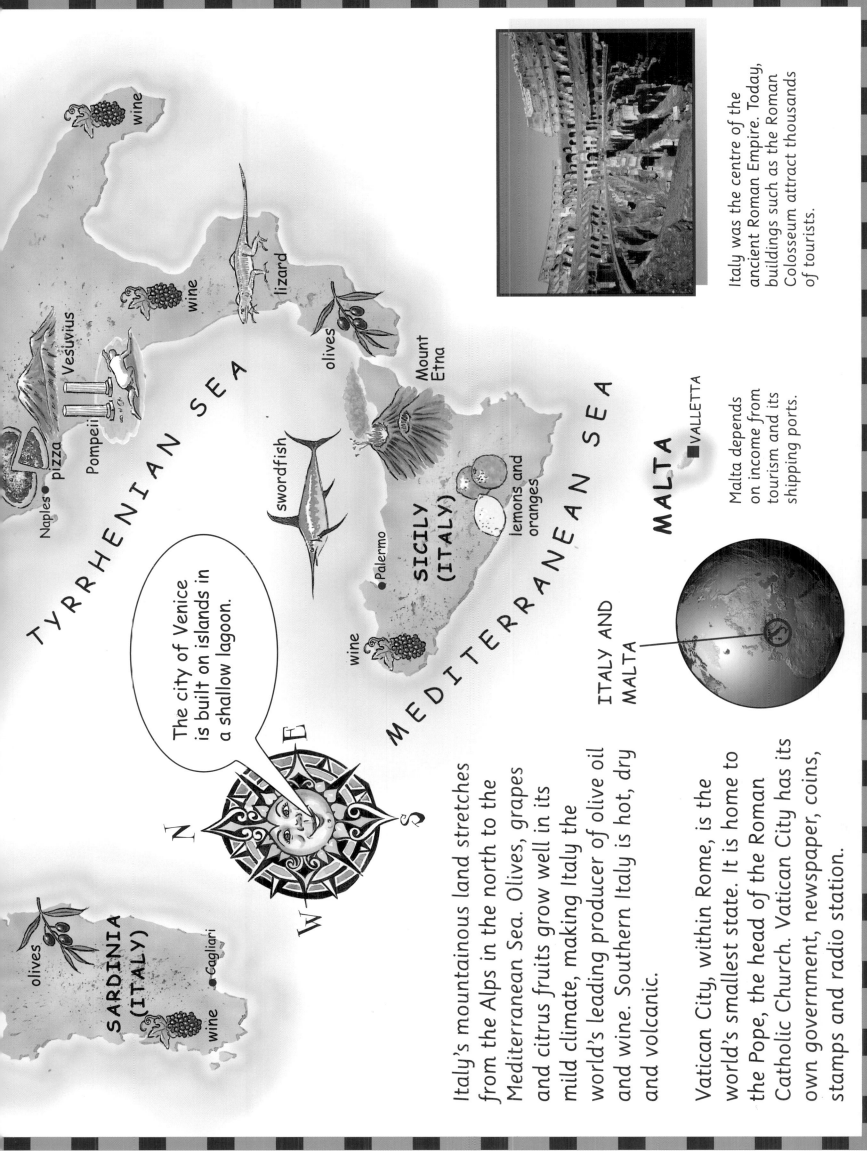

wine

wine

lizard

Vesuvius

Pompeii

olives

Naples • pizza

Mount Etna

swordfish

lemons and oranges

SICILY (ITALY)

Palermo •

TYRRHENIAN SEA

MEDITERRANEAN SEA

The city of Venice is built on islands in a shallow lagoon.

N E S W

wine

SARDINIA (ITALY)

olives

wine • Cagliari

Italy's mountainous land stretches from the Alps in the north to the Mediterranean Sea. Olives, grapes and citrus fruits grow well in its mild climate, making Italy the world's leading producer of olive oil and wine. Southern Italy is hot, dry and volcanic.

Vatican City, within Rome, is the world's smallest state. It is home to the Pope, the head of the Roman Catholic Church. Vatican City has its own government, newspaper, coins, stamps and radio station.

Italy was the centre of the ancient Roman Empire. Today, buildings such as the Roman Colosseum attract thousands of tourists.

MALTA

■ VALLETTA

Malta depends on income from tourism and its shipping ports.

ITALY AND MALTA

King Agamemnon's mask

olives

NAXOS

octopus

KOS

RHODES

THIRA

olives

wine

CRETE

• Irá Klion

dolphins

AEGEAN SEA

MEDITERRANEAN SEA

Greece and the Greek Islands

Greece is in southern Europe. It is a dry, mountainous country with many islands. The capital city, Athens, is home to more than one third of Greece's population. Farming and tourism are the major industries.

The Ancient Greeks were Europe's first great civilisation. Each year, thousands of tourists explore Greece's ancient buildings and archaeological sites. Greece is a popular holiday destination, attracting many visitors with its scenery, sunshine and fine beaches. Its hot climate is ideal for growing olives, grapes and citrus fruits.

The Parthenon is an ancient Greek temple. It stands on the Acropolis – a rocky hill that towers over the city of Athens.

The south of the region is rugged and mountainous with many areas of rich farmland. In 1993 Czechoslovakia split into two countries: the Czech Republic and Slovakia. Slovenia, Bosnia and Herzegovina, Croatia, and Macedonia were all once part of Yugoslavia, but have recently become independent countries.

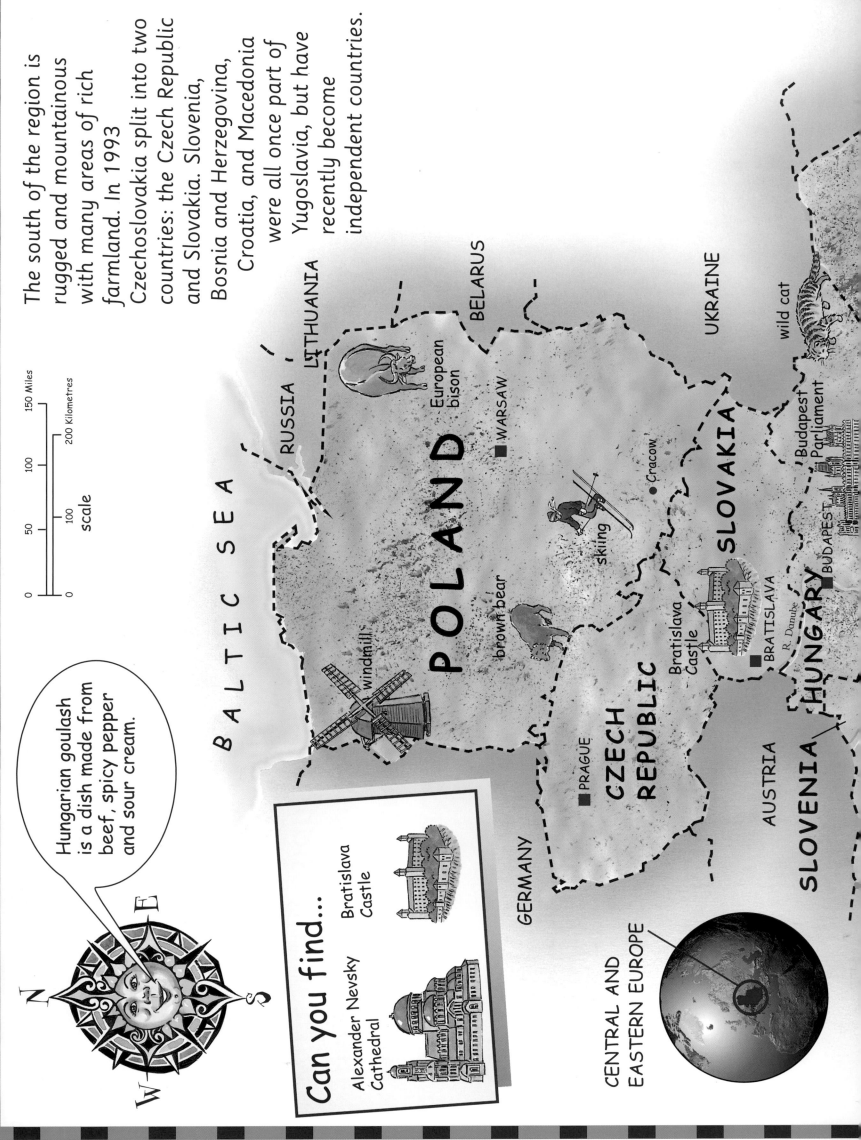

Hungarian goulash is a dish made from beef, spicy pepper and sour cream.

150 Miles
200 Kilometres
scale
0   50   100
0   100

BALTIC SEA

RUSSIA

LITHUANIA

BELARUS

POLAND

European bison

■ WARSAW

UKRAINE

• Cracow

skiing

brown bear

windmills

wild cat

SLOVAKIA

Bratislava Castle

■ BRATISLAVA

R. Danube

Budapest Parliament

■ BUDAPEST

■ PRAGUE

CZECH REPUBLIC

HUNGARY

GERMANY

AUSTRIA

SLOVENIA

Can you find...

Bratislava Castle

Alexander Nevsky Cathedral

CENTRAL AND EASTERN EUROPE

Central and Eastern Europe

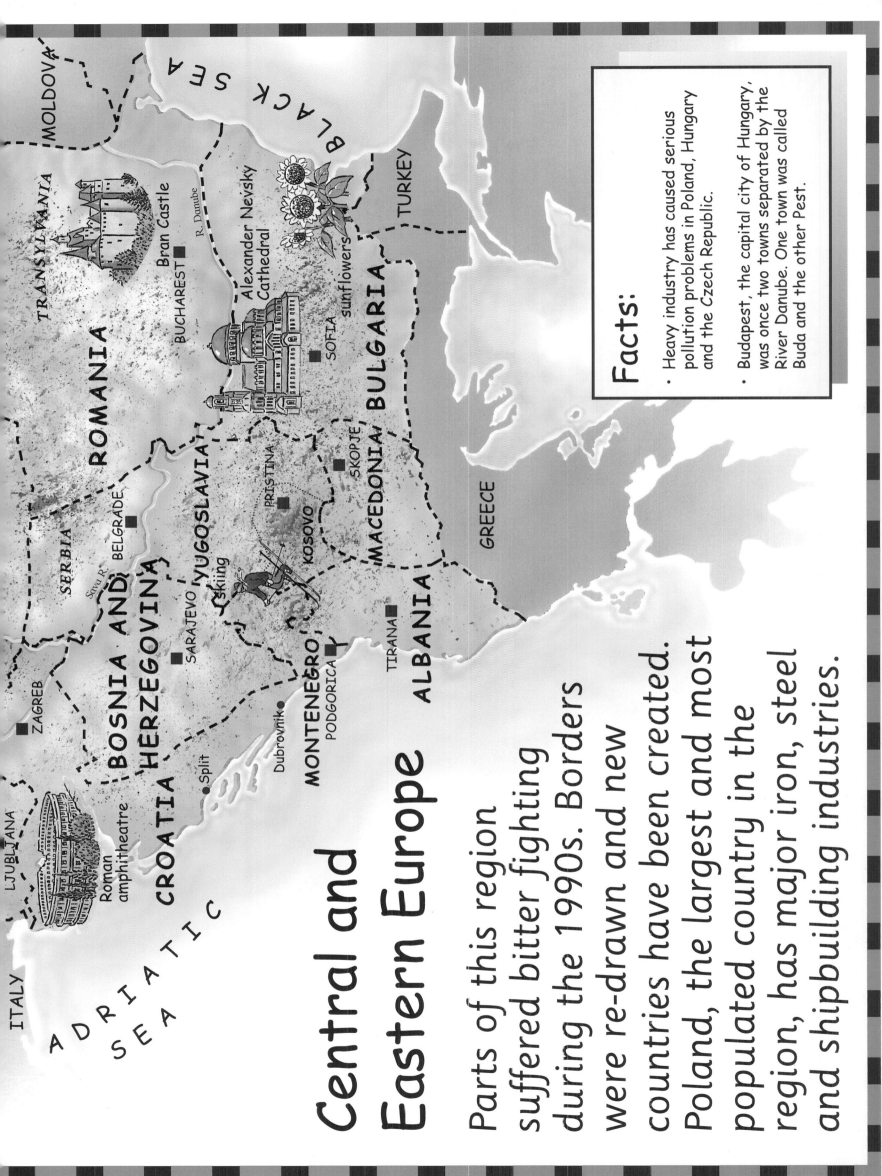

Parts of this region suffered bitter fighting during the 1990s. Borders were re-drawn and new countries have been created. Poland, the largest and most populated country in the region, has major iron, steel and shipbuilding industries.

Facts:

- Heavy industry has caused serious pollution problems in Poland, Hungary and the Czech Republic.

- Budapest, the capital city of Hungary, was once two towns separated by the River Danube. One town was called Buda and the other Pest.

Map labels

MOLDOVA

BLACK SEA

TRANSYLVANIA

Bran Castle

R. Danube

ROMANIA

BUCHAREST

Alexander Nevsky Cathedral

sunflowers

SOFIA

BULGARIA

TURKEY

MACEDONIA

SKOPJE

PRISTINA

KOSOVO

SERBIA

BELGRADE

Sava R.

YUGOSLAVIA

Skiing

BOSNIA AND HERZEGOVINA

SARAJEVO

MONTENEGRO,

PODGORICA

Dubrovnik

TIRANA

ALBANIA

GREECE

ZAGREB

CROATIA

Split

Roman amphitheatre

LJUBLJANA

ITALY

ADRIATIC SEA

Northern Eurasia

This vast region stretches across Asia and Europe. Until 1991 it was one single country, the Soviet Union. Today, it is made up of 15 independent nations including Russia, the largest country in the world.

NORTHERN EURASIA

BARENTS SEA

ice-breaker

polar bear

FINLAND

Winter Palace

TALLIN

ESTONIA

Kremlin

LATVIA

RIGA

RUSSIA

LITHUANIA

VILNIUS

woolly mammoth fossils

oil

POLAND

MINSK

BELARUS

MOSCOW

St. Basil's Cathedral

URAL MOUNTAINS

Fabergé egg

balalaika

Yenisey R.

SLOVAKIA

HUNGARY

MOLDOVA

KIEV

ROMANIA

UKRAINE

BULGARIA

Don R.

ballet

ox

BLACK SEA

caviar

nomad yurt

TURKEY

KAZAKHSTAN

CASPIAN SEA

ASTANA

TBILISI

GEORGIA

camel

snow leopard

YEREVAN

ARMENIA

BAKU

TASHKENT

CHINA

AZERBAIJAN

Turkmen horseman

UZBEKISTAN

BISHKEK

ASHGABAT

cotton

IRAN

KYRGYZSTAN

DUSHANBE

TURKMENISTAN

AFGHANISTAN

TAJIKISTAN

40

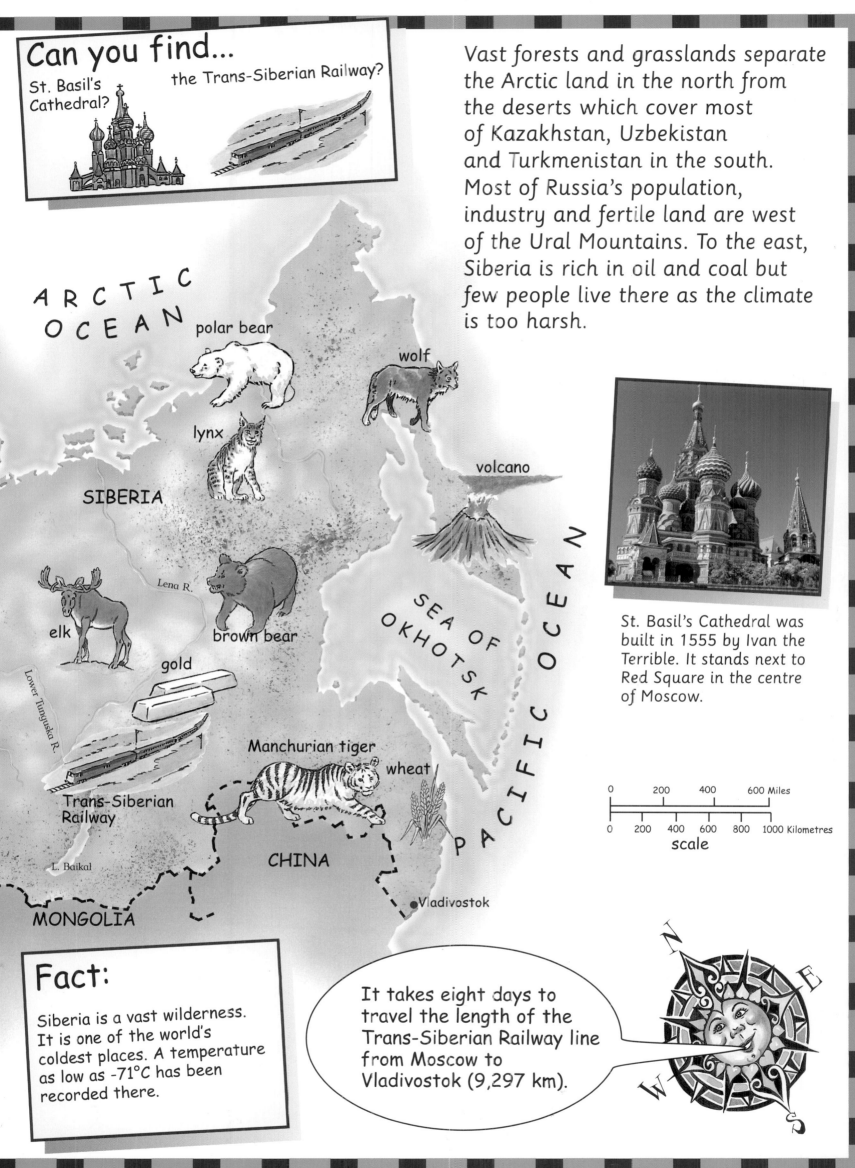

Can you find...

St. Basil's Cathedral?

the Trans-Siberian Railway?

Vast forests and grasslands separate the Arctic land in the north from the deserts which cover most of Kazakhstan, Uzbekistan and Turkmenistan in the south. Most of Russia's population, industry and fertile land are west of the Ural Mountains. To the east, Siberia is rich in oil and coal but few people live there as the climate is too harsh.

ARCTIC OCEAN

polar bear

wolf

lynx

volcano

SIBERIA

Lena R.

elk

brown bear

gold

Lower Tunguska R.

Manchurian tiger

wheat

Trans-Siberian Railway

SEA OF OKHOTSK

PACIFIC OCEAN

L. Baikal

CHINA

MONGOLIA

Vladivostok

St. Basil's Cathedral was built in 1555 by Ivan the Terrible. It stands next to Red Square in the centre of Moscow.

0	200	400	600 Miles
0	200 400 600	800	1000 Kilometres

scale

Fact:

Siberia is a vast wilderness. It is one of the world's coldest places. A temperature as low as -71°C has been recorded there.

It takes eight days to travel the length of the Trans-Siberian Railway line from Moscow to Vladivostok (9,297 km).

N E W S

Can you find...

the Royal Tomb at Petra?

the Suleymaniye Mosque?

BULGARIA

GREECE

BLACK SEA

• Istanbul

TURKEY

■ ANKARA

Suleymaniye Mosque

whirling dervish

Krak des Chevaliers

TURKISH STATE OF CYPRUS

NICOSIA

BEIRUT

CYPRUS

LEBANON

SYRIA

DAMASCUS

WEST BANK (disputed)

■ AMMAN

MEDITERRANEAN SEA

JERUSALEM

JORDAN

ISRAEL

Dead Sea

Dome of the Rock

EGYPT

Petra

scorpion

RED SEA

Mecca

Jeddah

SOUTH-WEST ASIA

South-West Asia

This area, also known as the Middle East, is mainly hot and dry with vast arid deserts to the south. It is a huge oil-producing region, supplying much of the world's oil.

The Middle East has long been troubled by wars between neighbouring countries. The discovery of large amounts of oil and natural gas around the Persian Gulf has brought great wealth to the region.

Fact:

The Dead Sea lies on the border of Israel and Jordan. Its water is so salty that people can float in it without swimming — it is impossible to sink.

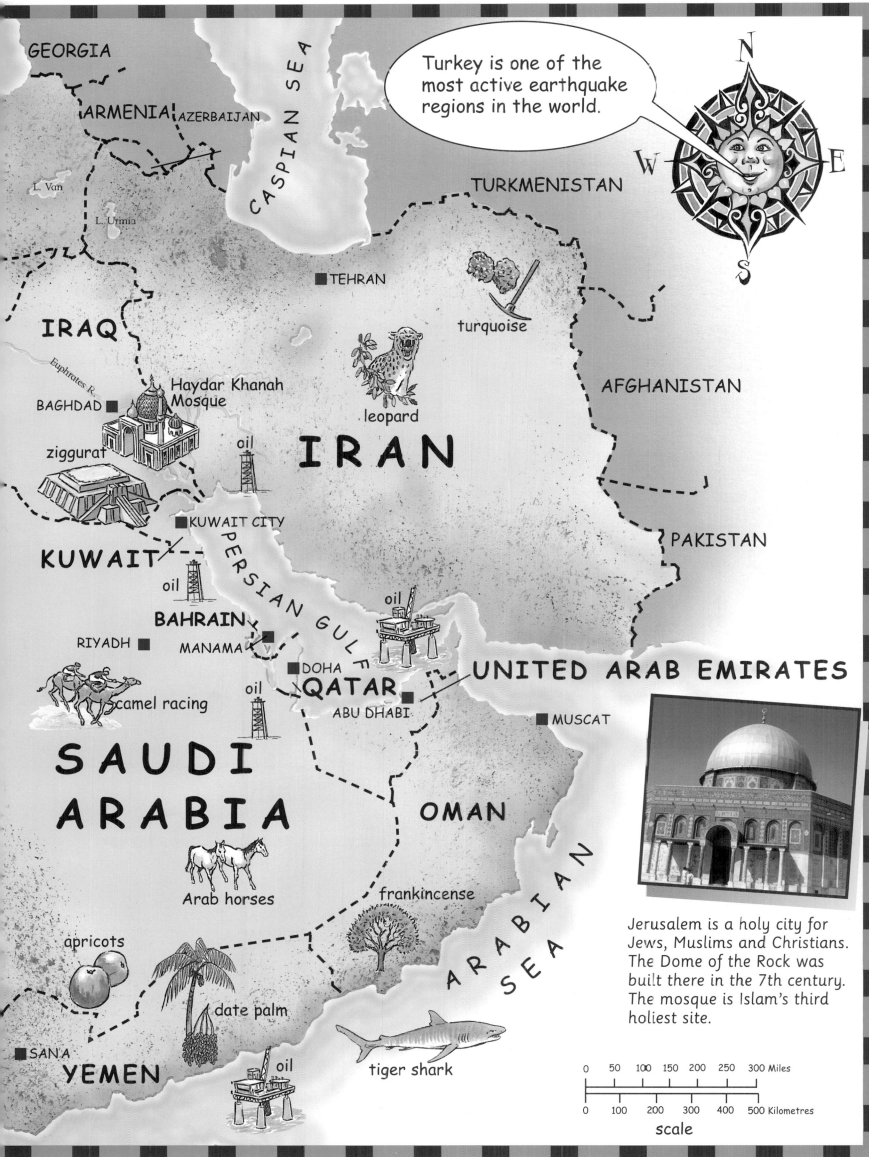

GEORGIA

ARMENIA AZERBAIJAN

CASPIAN SEA

L. Van

L. Urmia

Turkey is one of the most active earthquake regions in the world.

TURKMENISTAN

N
W E
S

TEHRAN

turquoise

leopard

AFGHANISTAN

IRAQ

Euphrates R.

BAGHDAD

Haydar Khanah Mosque

ziggurat

oil

IRAN

PAKISTAN

KUWAIT CITY

KUWAIT

oil

PERSIAN GULF

BAHRAIN

RIYADH

MANAMA

DOHA

oil

QATAR

oil

ABU DHABI

UNITED ARAB EMIRATES

MUSCAT

camel racing

SAUDI ARABIA

OMAN

ARABIAN SEA

Arab horses

apricots

frankincense

date palm

SAN'A

YEMEN

oil

tiger shark

Jerusalem is a holy city for Jews, Muslims and Christians. The Dome of the Rock was built there in the 7th century. The mosque is Islam's third holiest site.

0   50 100 150 200 250 300 Miles

0   100 200 300 400 500 Kilometres

scale

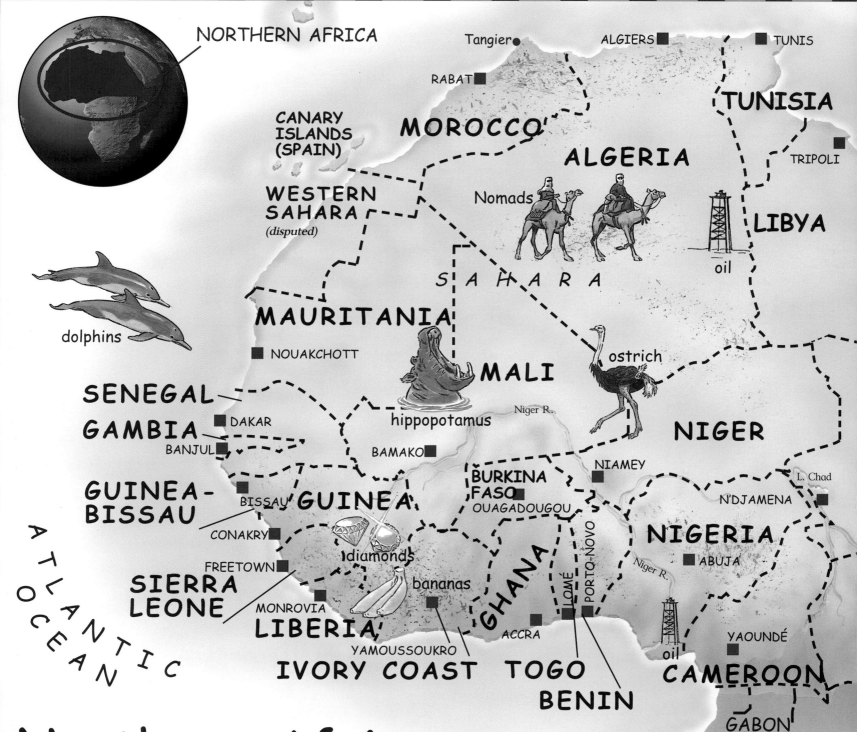

NORTHERN AFRICA

Tangier• ALGIERS ■ ■ TUNIS

RABAT ■ **TUNISIA**

CANARY ISLANDS (SPAIN)

MOROCCO

TRIPOLI

ALGERIA

WESTERN SAHARA
(disputed)

Nomads

LIBYA

oil

S A H A R A

MAURITANIA

NOUAKCHOTT

ostrich

MALI

dolphins

hippopotamus

Niger R.

NIGER

SENEGAL

GAMBIA DAKAR ■

BANJUL ■ BAMAKO ■

NIAMEY ■

L. Chad

N'DJAMENA ■

GUINEA-BISSAU

BISSAU ■

GUINEA

CONAKRY ■

diamonds

BURKINA FASO ■

OUAGADOUGOU

NIGERIA

Niger R.

ABUJA ■

SIERRA LEONE

FREETOWN ■

bananas

GHANA

LOMÉ

PORTO-NOVO

IVORY COAST

MONROVIA ■

LIBERIA

YAMOUSSOUKRO

ACCRA ■

TOGO

BENIN

oil

YAOUNDÉ ■

CAMEROON

A T L A N T I C   O C E A N

GABON ■

Northern Africa

Much of the huge continent of Africa is hot and dry. The land along the Mediterranean coast and the Nile Valley is rich and fertile. The vast Sahara Desert covers more than half of north Africa.

Fact:

The Sahara Desert is the largest desert in the world, covering about nine million square kilometres.

Many Africans live in small villages and farm the land. The Nile Valley in Egypt is the most densely populated region. Cairo is Africa's largest city.

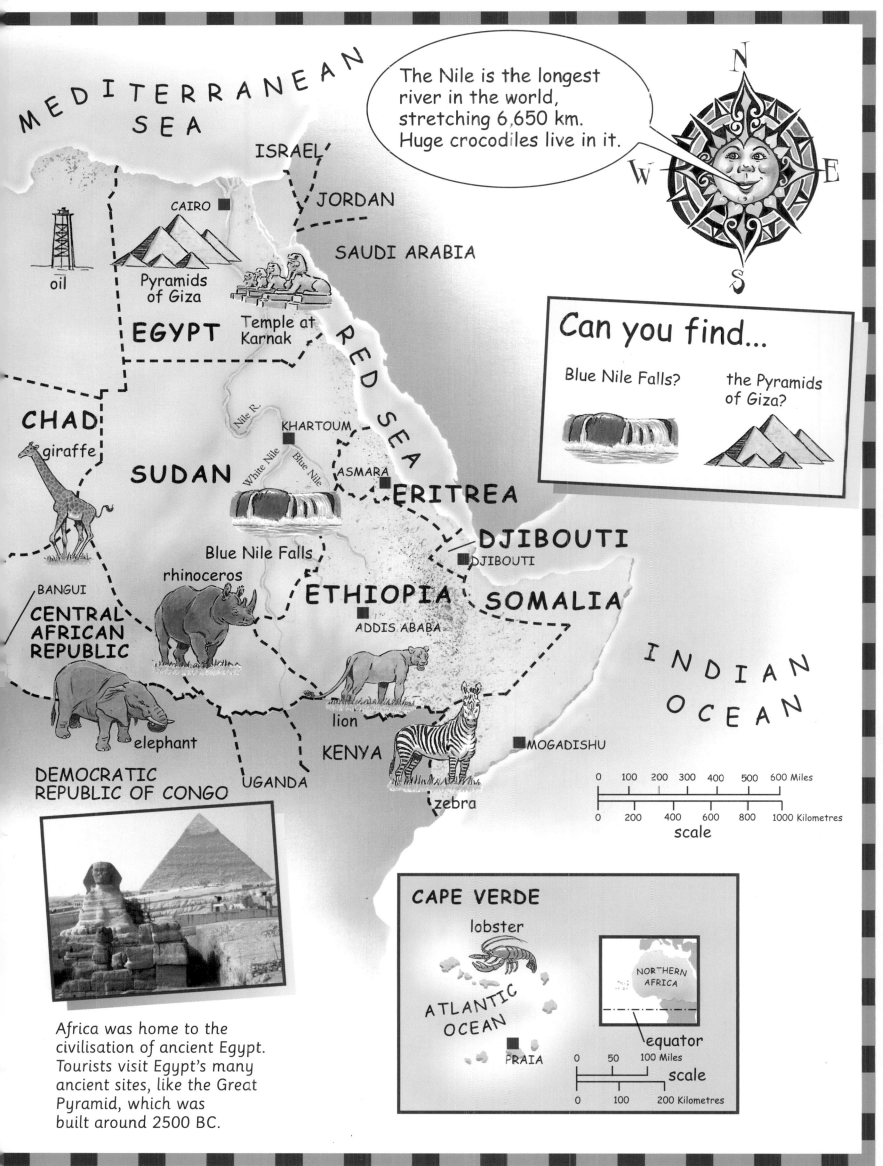

MEDITERRANEAN SEA

The Nile is the longest river in the world, stretching 6,650 km. Huge crocodiles live in it.

N
W E
S

ISRAEL

JORDAN

CAIRO

SAUDI ARABIA

Pyramids of Giza

Temple at Karnak

EGYPT

oil

RED SEA

Can you find...

Blue Nile Falls?   the Pyramids of Giza?

CHAD

giraffe

Nile R.

KHARTOUM

SUDAN

White Nile   Blue Nile

ASMARA

ERITREA

DJIBOUTI

DJIBOUTI

Blue Nile Falls

rhinoceros

ETHIOPIA

SOMALIA

ADDIS ABABA

BANGUI

CENTRAL AFRICAN REPUBLIC

INDIAN OCEAN

lion

elephant

KENYA

MOGADISHU

DEMOCRATIC REPUBLIC OF CONGO

UGANDA

zebra

0   100 200 300 400 500 600 Miles

0   200 400 600 800 1000 Kilometres

scale

Africa was home to the civilisation of ancient Egypt. Tourists visit Egypt's many ancient sites, like the Great Pyramid, which was built around 2500 BC.

CAPE VERDE

lobster

NORTHERN AFRICA

ATLANTIC OCEAN

equator

PRAIA

0   50   100 Miles

0   100 200 Kilometres

scale

The top of Mount Kilimanjaro in Tanzania is covered in snow all year round.

Southern Africa

The mighty Congo River runs through dense, tropical rainforests in Central Africa. Crocodiles, chimpanzees and gorillas live in these hot, steamy forests. Grasslands and deserts make up much of Southern Africa, but there is rich farmland in the far south.

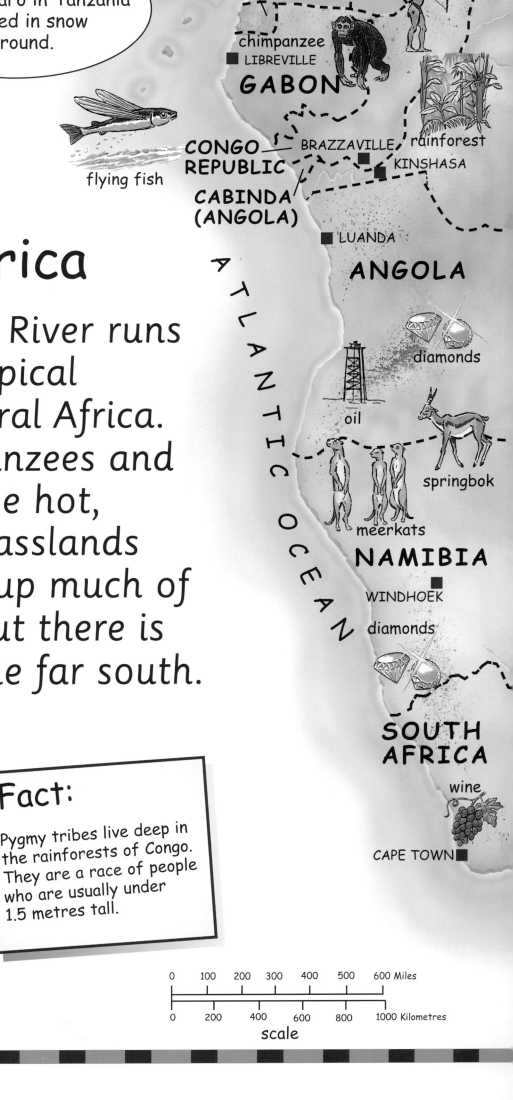

EQUATORIAL GUINEA

pygmies

MALABO

CAMEROON

chimpanzee LIBREVILLE

GABON

rainforest

flying fish

CONGO REPUBLIC

BRAZZAVILLE

KINSHASA

CABINDA (ANGOLA)

LUANDA

ANGOLA

ATLANTIC OCEAN

diamonds

oil

springbok

meerkats

NAMIBIA

WINDHOEK

diamonds

SOUTH AFRICA

wine

CAPE TOWN

Can you find...

Victoria Falls?

meerkats?

Fact:

Pygmy tribes live deep in the rainforests of Congo. They are a race of people who are usually under 1.5 metres tall.

0   100   200   300   400   500   600 Miles

0   200   400   600   800   1000 Kilometres

scale

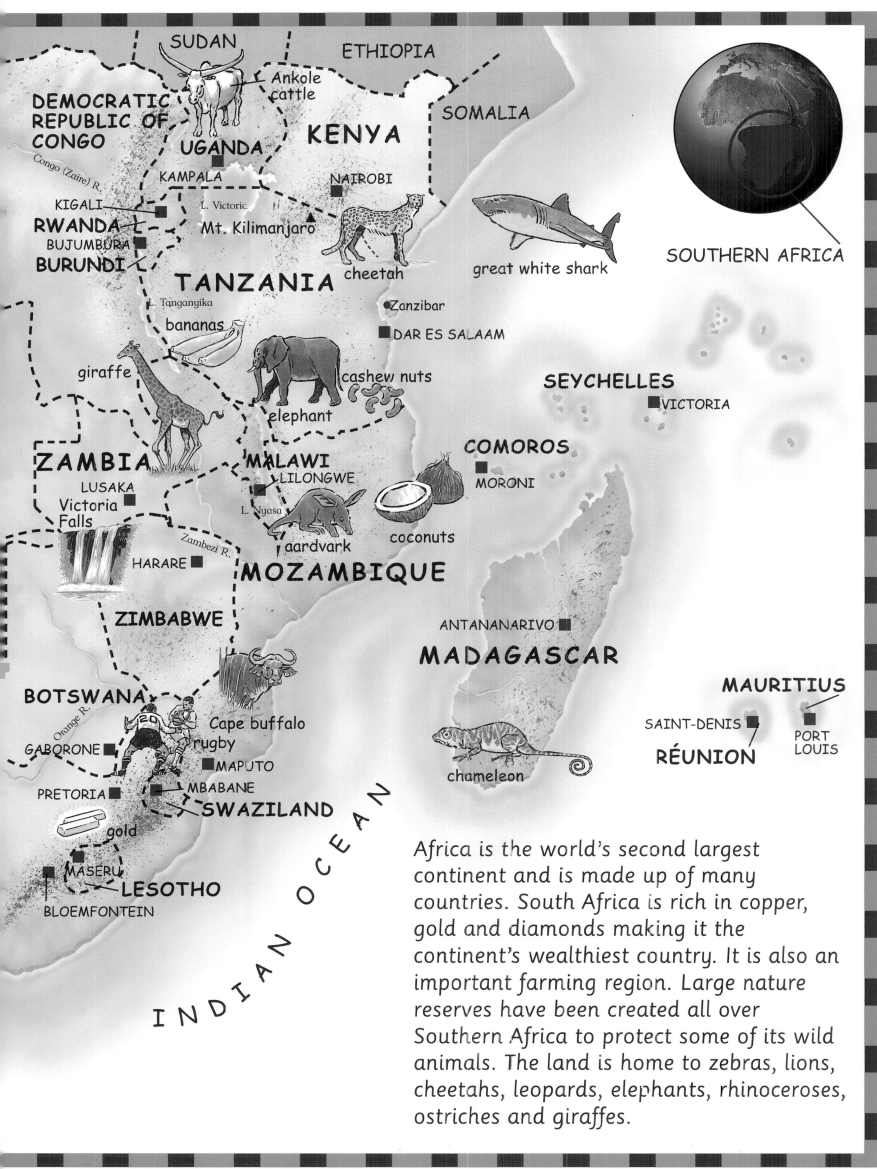

SUDAN

ETHIOPIA

Ankole cattle

DEMOCRATIC REPUBLIC OF CONGO

SOMALIA

KENYA

Congo (Zaire) R.

UGANDA

KAMPALA

NAIROBI

L. Victoria

KIGALI

RWANDA

Mt. Kilimanjaro

cheetah

great white shark

BUJUMBURA

BURUNDI

TANZANIA

SOUTHERN AFRICA

L. Tanganyika

Zanzibar

bananas

DAR ES SALAAM

giraffe

cashew nuts

SEYCHELLES

VICTORIA

elephant

COMOROS

ZAMBIA

MALAWI

LILONGWE

MORONI

LUSAKA

L. Nyasa

Victoria Falls

aardvark

coconuts

Zambezi R.

HARARE

MOZAMBIQUE

ANTANANARIVO

ZIMBABWE

MADAGASCAR

MAURITIUS

Cape buffalo

BOTSWANA

rugby

SAINT-DENIS

PORT LOUIS

Orange R.

GABORONE

MAPUTO

chameleon

RÉUNION

PRETORIA

MBABANE

SWAZILAND

gold

MASERU

LESOTHO

BLOEMFONTEIN

INDIAN OCEAN

Africa is the world's second largest continent and is made up of many countries. South Africa is rich in copper, gold and diamonds making it the continent's wealthiest country. It is also an important farming region. Large nature reserves have been created all over Southern Africa to protect some of its wild animals. The land is home to zebras, lions, cheetahs, leopards, elephants, rhinoceroses, ostriches and giraffes.

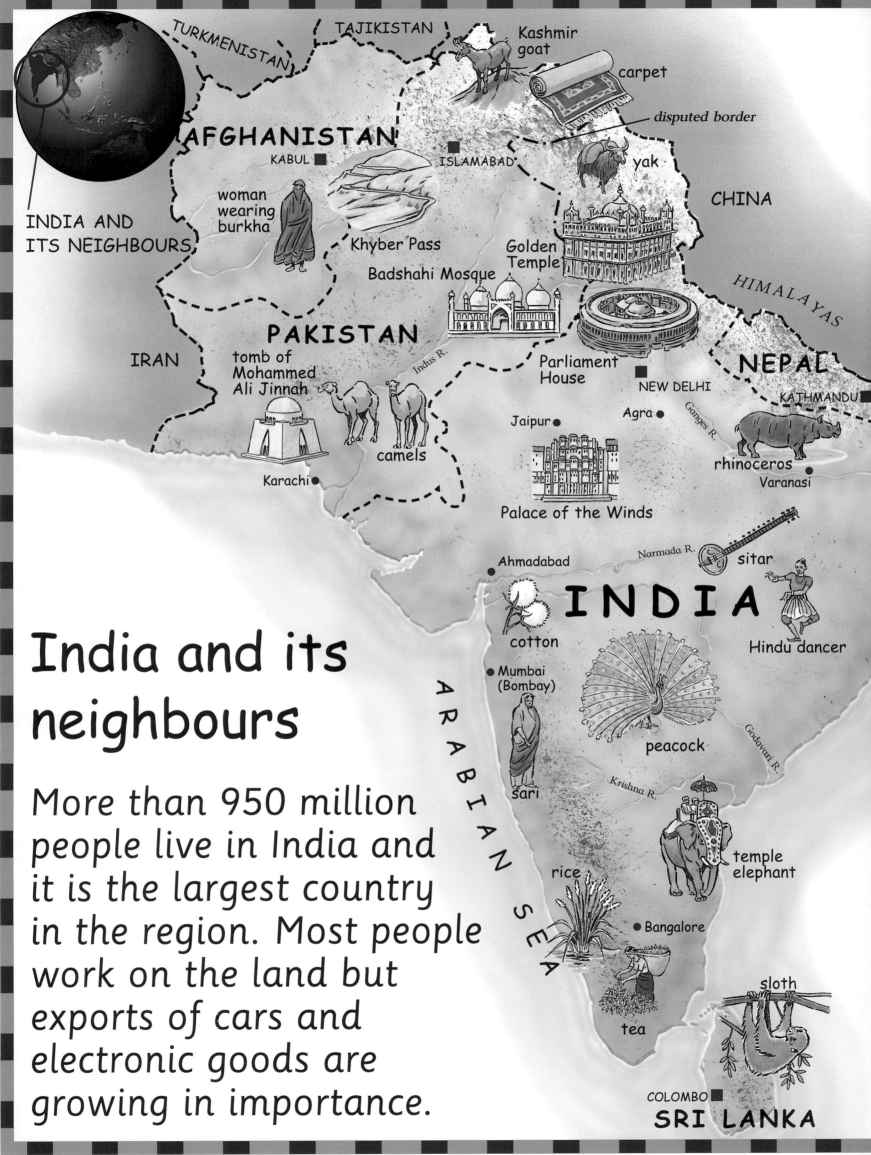

TURKMENISTAN

TAJIKISTAN

Kashmir goat

carpet

disputed border

AFGHANISTAN

KABUL

ISLAMABAD

yak

CHINA

woman wearing burkha

Khyber Pass

Badshahi Mosque

Golden Temple

HIMALAYAS

PAKISTAN

IRAN

tomb of Mohammed Ali Jinnah

Indus R.

Parliament House

NEW DELHI

NEPAL

KATHMANDU

camels

Jaipur

Agra

Ganges R.

rhinoceros

Karachi

Palace of the Winds

Varanasi

Narmada R.

sitar

Ahmadabad

INDIA

cotton

Hindu dancer

A
R
A
B
I
A
N
   S
E
A

Mumbai (Bombay)

peacock

Godavari R.

sari

Krishna R.

rice

temple elephant

Bangalore

sloth

tea

COLOMBO

SRI LANKA

India and its neighbours

More than 950 million people live in India and it is the largest country in the region. Most people work on the land but exports of cars and electronic goods are growing in importance.

Can you find...

the Palace of the Winds?

the Golden Temple?

a temple elephant?

Vast mountain ranges separate this region from Central Asia. The climate is hot and dry, so many people live on the coast or on the fertile plains along the Ganges and Indus rivers. India, Bangladesh and Sri Lanka are some of the world's main tea-growing nations. Most industries are concentrated in India and Pakistan's large, crowded cities.

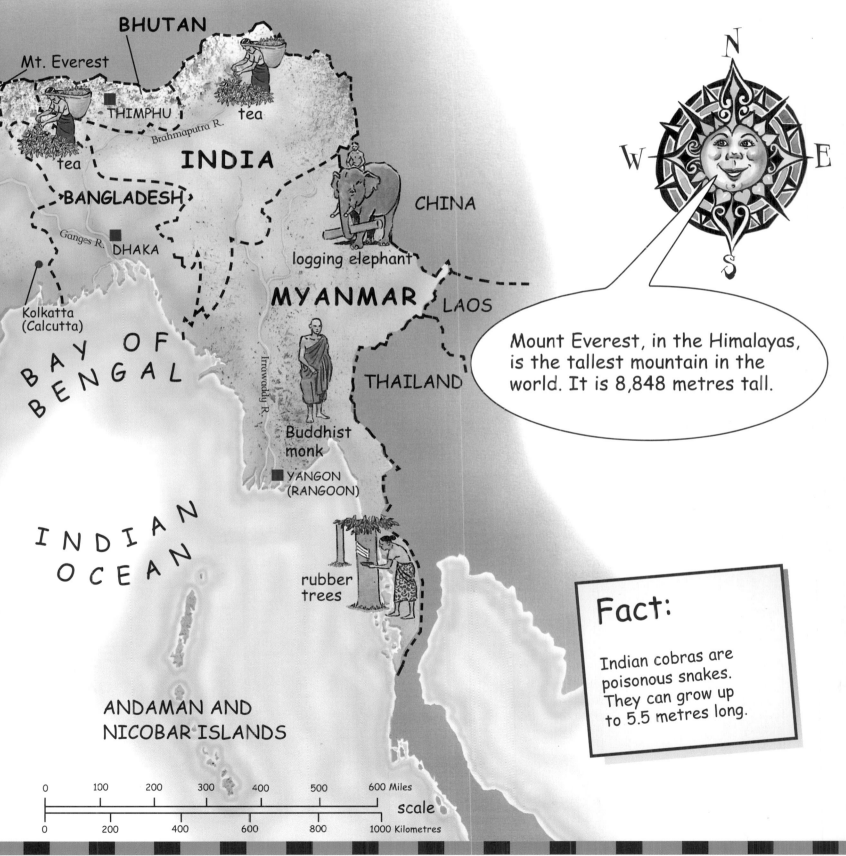

BHUTAN

Mt. Everest

THIMPHU

tea

Brahmaputra R.

tea

INDIA

BANGLADESH

Ganges R.

DHAKA

CHINA

logging elephant

Kolkatta (Calcutta)

MYANMAR

LAOS

BAY OF BENGAL

Irrawaddy R.

THAILAND

Buddhist monk

INDIAN OCEAN

YANGON (RANGOON)

rubber trees

ANDAMAN AND NICOBAR ISLANDS

Mount Everest, in the Himalayas, is the tallest mountain in the world. It is 8,848 metres tall.

Fact:

Indian cobras are poisonous snakes. They can grow up to 5.5 metres long.

| 0 | 100 | 200 | 300 | 400 | 500 | 600 Miles |
scale
| 0 | 200 | 400 | 600 | 800 | 1000 Kilometres |

Japan

Japan is made up of four large islands and thousands of smaller ones. It lies off the east coast of China. Japan's cities are built along its flat coastland because mountains and forests cover much of the country inland.

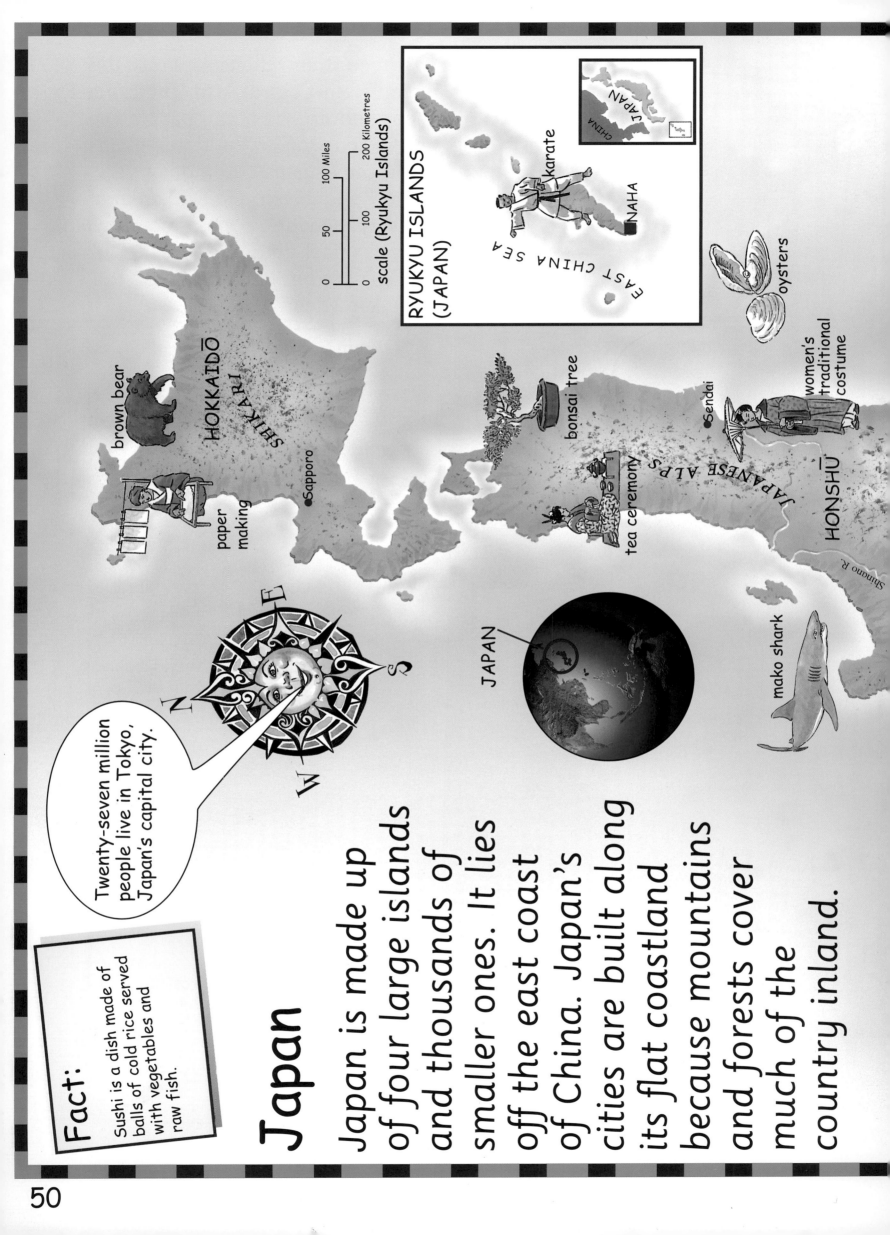

Twenty-seven million people live in Tokyo, Japan's capital city.

Fact:

Sushi is a dish made of cold rice served balls of cold rice served with vegetables and raw fish.

RYUKYU ISLANDS (JAPAN)

karate

NAHA

EAST CHINA SEA

CHINA

JAPAN

scale (Ryukyu Islands)

200 Kilometres

100 Miles

100

50

HOKKAIDŌ

SHIKARI

brown bear

Sapporo

paper making

bonsai tree

tea ceremony

Sendai

JAPANESE ALPS

HONSHŪ

women's traditional costume

oysters

Shinano R.

mako shark

JAPAN

N E S W

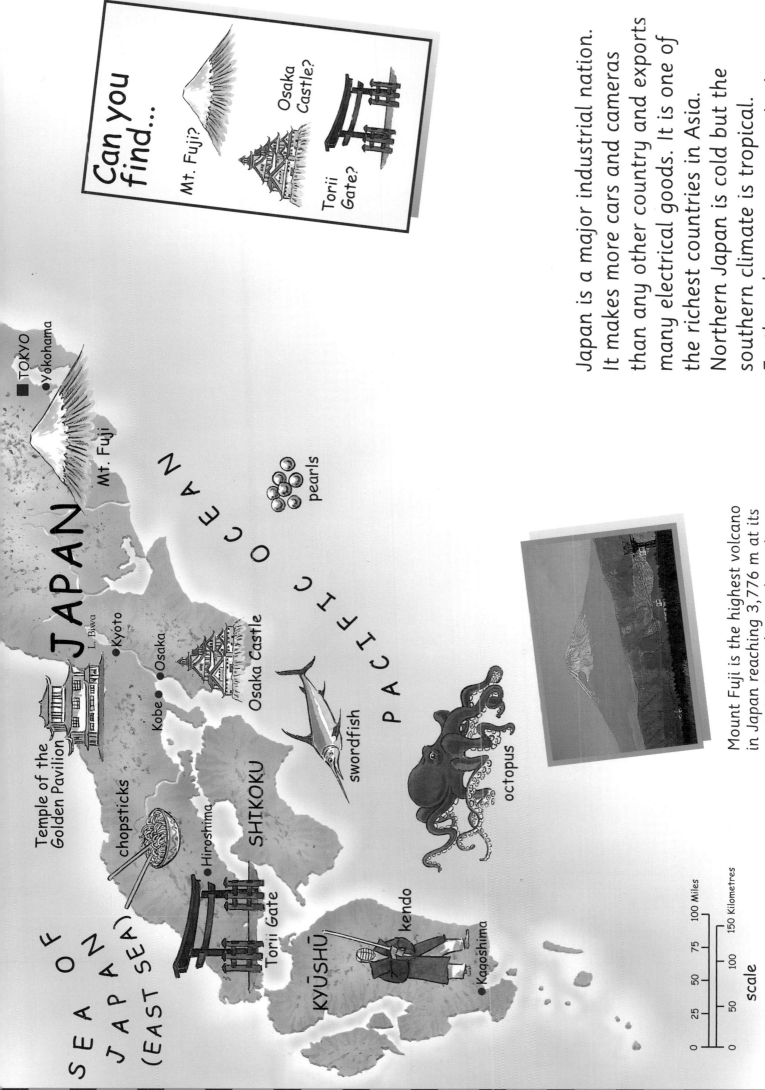

Can you find...

Mt. Fuji?

Osaka Castle?

Torii Gate?

Japan is a major industrial nation. It makes more cars and cameras than any other country and exports many electrical goods. It is one of the richest countries in Asia. Northern Japan is cold but the southern climate is tropical. Earthquakes are common in Japan and the country is often hit by fierce storms called typhoons.

Mount Fuji is the highest volcano in Japan reaching 3,776 m at its summit. According to legend, an earthquake created Mt. Fuji in 286 BC. Its last big eruption was in 1707.

■TOKYO
•Yokohama

Mt. Fuji

pearls

JAPAN

Temple of the Golden Pavilion

chopsticks

L. Biwa

•Kyoto

Kobe•
•Osaka

Osaka Castle

SEA OF JAPAN (EAST SEA)

•Hiroshima

SHIKOKU

swordfish

PACIFIC OCEAN

Torii Gate

KYŪSHŪ

kendo

octopus

•Kagoshima

scale

0   25   50   75   100 Miles

0   50   100   150 Kilometres

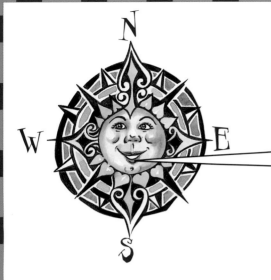

Oil-rich Brunei is one of the world's smallest and wealthiest countries.

Southeast Asia

Southeast Asia is made up of two small areas of mainland and almost 20,000 islands. The climate is hot and humid. Tropical rainforests cover much of this mountainous region and provide the world with most of its hardwoods.

Can you find...

Angkor Wat?   the skyscrapers of Singapore?

SOUTHEAST ASIA

tiger shark

swordfish

MANILA

PHILIPPINES

pineapple

MINDANAO

In remote areas of Southeast Asia people live in houses raised on stilts to avoid being flooded during the rainy season. Monsoon rains fall from June to October. The climate is ideal for growing rice, Southeast Asia's main crop. Pineapples, bananas, mangoes and coconuts are also grown.
The rainforests are rich in plantlife and are home to orang-utans, rhinoceroses, leopards and tigers.

BRUNEI
BANDAR SERI BEGAWAN

MALAYSIA

head hunter with blowpipe

BORNEO

nice

CELEBES

coffee

coconuts

oil rig

house on stilts

PACIFIC OCEAN

| 0 | 100 | 200 | 300 | 400 | 500 | 600 Miles |

| 0 | 200 | 400 | 600 | 800 | 1000 Kilometres |

scale

IRIAN JAYA

PAPUA NEW GUINEA

INDONESIA

Borobudur Temple

shadow puppet

Komodo dragon

TIMOR

hammerhead shark

AUSTRALIA

China, Mongolia, Korea and Taiwan

CHINA, MONGOLIA, KOREA AND TAIWAN

More people live in China than in any other country on Earth. Most of the population farm the fertile land in the east, growing rice, wheat, maize and tea. China is also an industrial nation and has many large cities.

High mountain ranges separate China from India and there are vast deserts to the north. The Korean peninsula is divided into North and South Korea. South Korea and the island of Taiwan have successful industries including textiles, cars and electrical goods.

KAZAKHSTAN

oil

wheat

KYRGYZSTAN

cotton

TAJIKISTAN

jade

PAKISTAN

giant panda

INDIA

XIZANG (TIBET)

Tibetan monk

HIMALAYAS

NEPAL

BHUTAN

INDIA

The Great Wall of China is 3,460 km long. It is the only man-made structure that can be seen from the Moon.

Can you find...

the Forbidden City?

the Potala Palace?

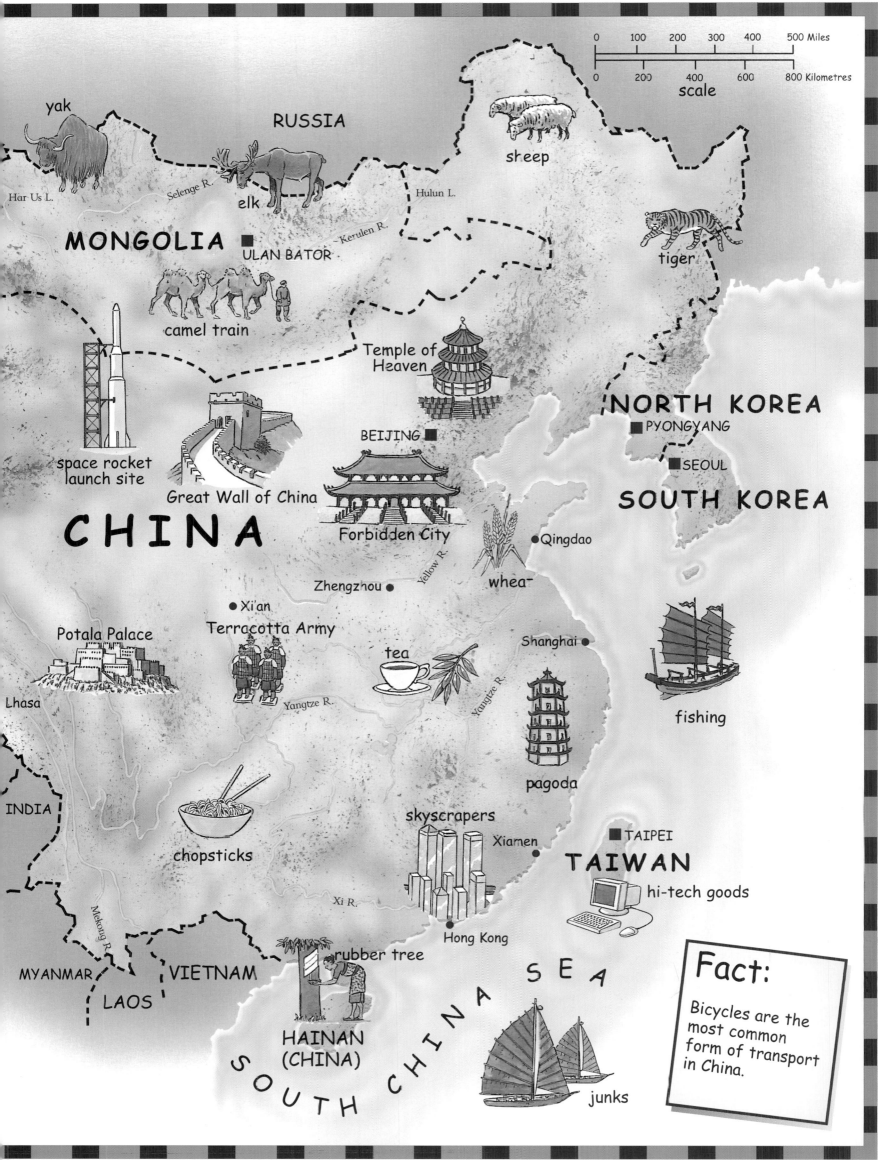

yak

RUSSIA

500 Miles
0 100 200 300 400
scale
0 200 400 600 800 Kilometres

sheep

Har Us L.
Selenge R.
elk
Hulun L.

tiger

MONGOLIA ■ ULAN BATOR

Kerulen R.

camel train

Temple of Heaven

NORTH KOREA
■ PYONGYANG

space rocket launch site

Great Wall of China

BEIJING ■

■ SEOUL

SOUTH KOREA

CHINA

Forbidden City

Qingdao

wheat

Zhengzhou ●

Yellow R.

Potala Palace

● Xi'an
Terracotta Army

tea

Shanghai ●

Lhasa

Yangtze R.

Yangtze R.

pagoda

fishing

INDIA

chopsticks

skyscrapers

Xiamen ●

■ TAIPEI

TAIWAN

hi-tech goods

Xi R.

Hong Kong ●

MYANMAR

VIETNAM

rubber tree

LAOS

Mekong R.

HAINAN (CHINA)

S O U T H   C H I N A   S E A

junks

Fact:

Bicycles are the most common form of transport in China.

AUSTRALIA AND
PAPUA NEW GUINEA

Papua New Guinea has over 700 languages – more than any other country.

traditional dancer

gold

■ PORT MORESBY

PAPUA NEW GUINEA

| 0 | 100 | 200 | 300 | 400 | 500 | 600 Miles |

| 0 | 200 | 400 | 600 | 800 | 1000 Kilometres |

scale (Papua New Guinea)

AUSTRALIA

Australia and Papua New Guinea

Australia is the world's smallest continent. It is a large, wealthy country with a small population. It is hot and dry inland so most people live in large coastal cities. Australia's wealth comes from farming and mining.

Central Australia is called the 'outback'. It is mainly deserts and grasslands. Few people live there, but vast numbers of sheep and cattle graze on stations (farms). Australia produces more wool than any other country. It also has large deposits of opals, diamonds, gold and silver.

INDIAN OCEAN

pearls

baobab tree

emu

Aboriginal dancers

WESTERN AUSTRALIA

red kangaroo

dingo

gold

cricket

Perth ●

| 0 | 100 | 200 | 300 | 400 | 500 | 600 Miles |

| 0 | 200 | 400 | 600 | 800 | 1000 Kilometres |

scale

Can you find...

Sydney Opera House?

Ayers Rock (Uluru)?

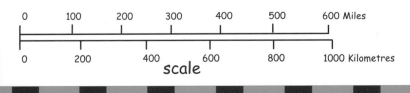

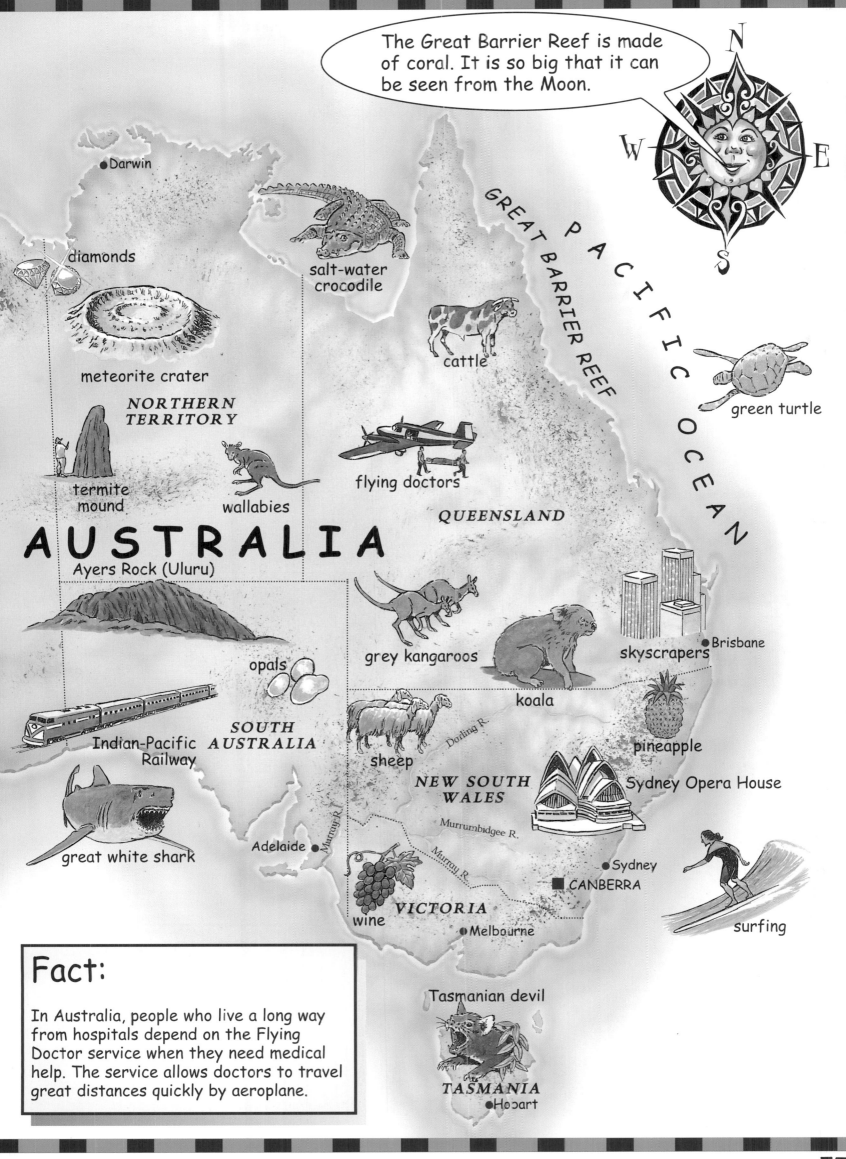

The Great Barrier Reef is made of coral. It is so big that it can be seen from the Moon.

•Darwin

diamonds

meteorite crater

salt-water crocodile

cattle

green turtle

NORTHERN TERRITORY

termite mound

wallabies

flying doctors

QUEENSLAND

AUSTRALIA

Ayers Rock (Uluru)

grey kangaroos

koala

skyscrapers

•Brisbane

opals

pineapple

Indian-Pacific Railway

SOUTH AUSTRALIA

sheep

Darling R.

NEW SOUTH WALES

Sydney Opera House

great white shark

Adelaide•

Murray R.

Murrumbidgee R.

Murray R.

•Sydney

■ CANBERRA

surfing

wine

VICTORIA

•Melbourne

Fact:

In Australia, people who live a long way from hospitals depend on the Flying Doctor service when they need medical help. The service allows doctors to travel great distances quickly by aeroplane.

Tasmanian devil

TASMANIA

•Hobart

New Zealand

New Zealand is divided into two islands. Most people live on its volcanic North Island. It has large cattle and sheep ranches and exports dairy produce and lamb.

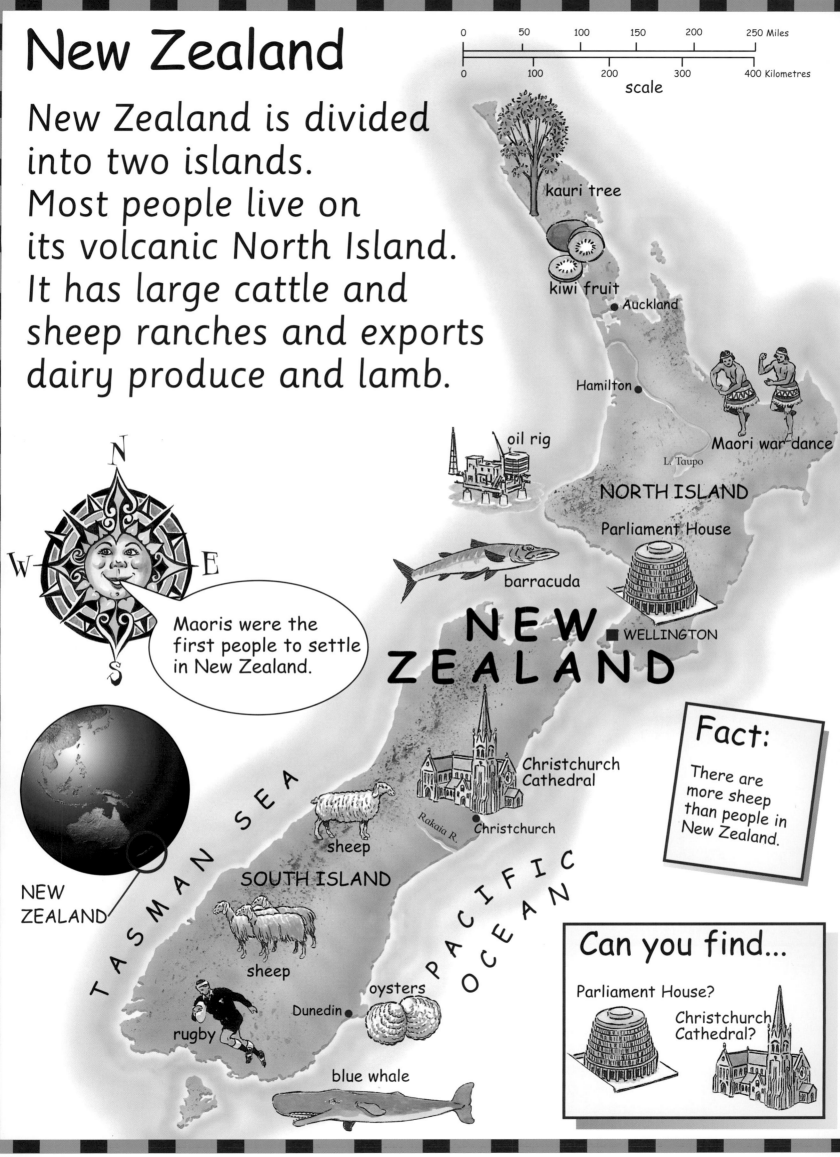

kauri tree

kiwi fruit

Auckland

Hamilton

oil rig

Maori war dance

L. Taupo

NORTH ISLAND

Parliament House

barracuda

N E W ZEALAND

■ WELLINGTON

Maoris were the first people to settle in New Zealand.

NEW ZEALAND

T A S M A N   S E A

Christchurch Cathedral

Rakaia R.

Christchurch

sheep

SOUTH ISLAND

sheep

rugby

Dunedin

oysters

blue whale

P A C I F I C   O C E A N

Fact:

There are more sheep than people in New Zealand.

Can you find...

Parliament House?

Christchurch Cathedral?

South Western Pacific Islands

Thousands of small tropical islands are scattered across the Pacific Ocean, east of Australia. Most islanders live in small villages. They fish and grow tropical fruit, including bananas and coconuts.

VANUATU

BANKS ISLANDS

scuba diving

great white shark

PORT VILA

LOYALTY ISLANDS

Yasur volcano

coconuts

NOUMÉA

NEW CALEDONIA (FRANCE)

SAMOAN ISLANDS

WESTERN SAMOA

bottlenosed dolphin

coconuts

APIA

manta ray

AMERICAN SAMOA (USA)

BOUGAINVILLE

house on stilts

NEW GEORGIA ISLANDS

HONIARA

bananas

SANTA CRUZ ISLANDS

SOLOMON ISLANDS

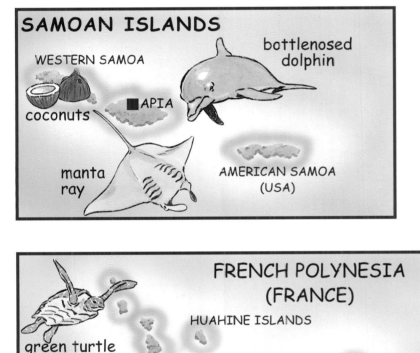

FRENCH POLYNESIA (FRANCE)

HUAHINE ISLANDS

green turtle

LEEWARD ISLANDS

pearls

bananas

Fact:

The people of Bougainville in the Solomon Islands have discovered how to use coconut oil as a fuel for motor cars.

0   100   200   300 Miles

scale

0   100   200   300   400   500 Kilometres

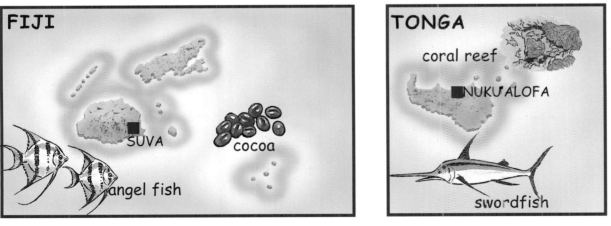

FIJI

SUVA

cocoa

angel fish

TONGA

coral reef

NUKU'ALOFA

swordfish

SOUTH WESTERN PACIFIC ISLANDS

The Arctic

The Arctic Ocean is covered in thick ice at the North Pole. The Inuit and Sami are the only people who live in this harsh environment, but many animals and plants survive there.

THE ARCTIC

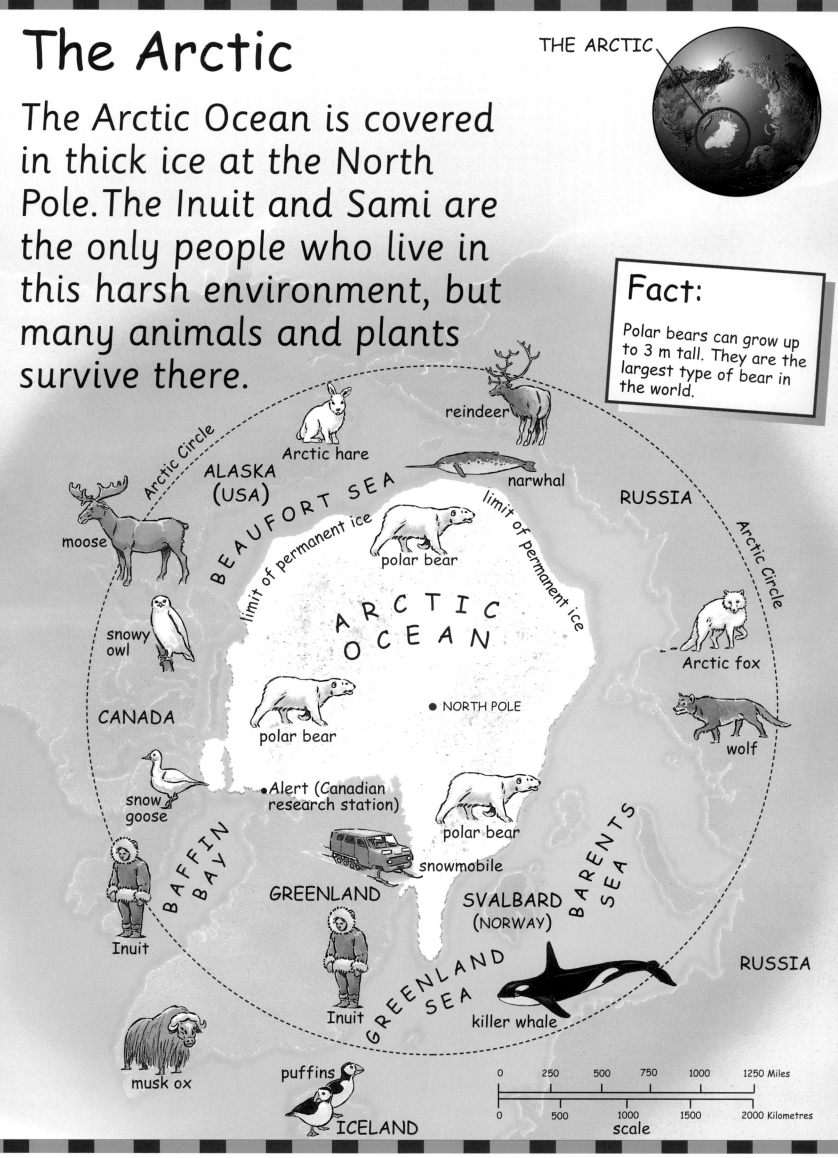

Arctic Circle

reindeer

Arctic hare

ALASKA
(USA)

narwhal

RUSSIA

moose

BEAUFORT SEA

limit of permanent ice

polar bear

limit of permanent ice

Arctic Circle

ARCTIC
OCEAN

snowy
owl

Arctic fox

polar bear

• NORTH POLE

wolf

CANADA

snow
goose

•Alert (Canadian
research station)

polar bear

BAFFIN
BAY

snowmobile

BARENTS
SEA

Inuit

GREENLAND

SVALBARD
(NORWAY)

Inuit

GREENLAND
SEA

RUSSIA

musk ox

puffins

killer whale

ICELAND

scale

0	250	500	750	1000	1250 Miles

0	500	1000	1500	2000 Kilometres

The Antarctic

The South Pole in the Antarctic is the coldest place on Earth. No country owns this frozen continent but many have set up scientific research stations there.

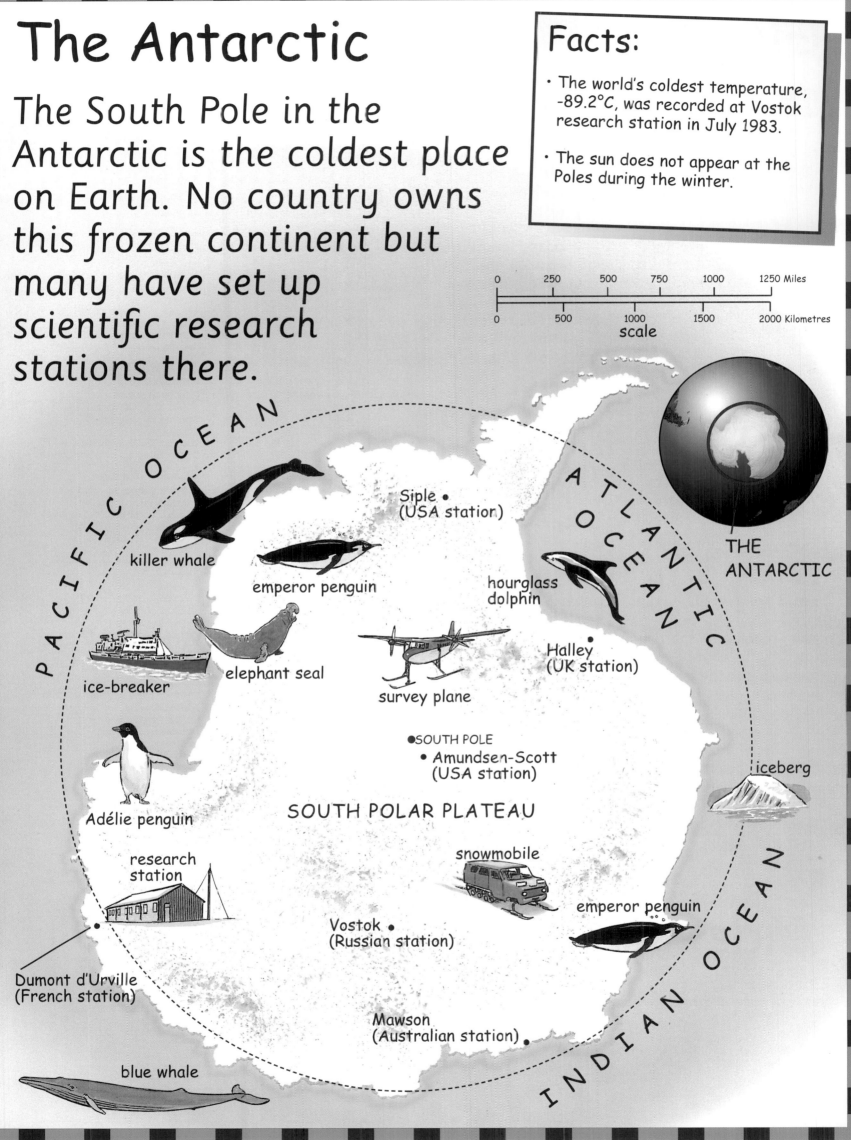

scale

0   250   500   750   1000   1250 Miles
0   500   1000   1500   2000 Kilometres

PACIFIC OCEAN

ATLANTIC OCEAN

INDIAN OCEAN

THE ANTARCTIC

killer whale

emperor penguin

hourglass dolphin

Siple (USA station)

Halley (UK station)

ice-breaker

elephant seal

survey plane

SOUTH POLE
Amundsen-Scott (USA station)

iceberg

Adélie penguin

SOUTH POLAR PLATEAU

research station

snowmobile

emperor penguin

Vostok (Russian station)

Dumont d'Urville (French station)

Mawson (Australian station)

blue whale

Glossary

climate The average weather of a region.

continent One of the large masses of land on the Earth's surface.

desert An area that has very little or no rainfall.

equator The imaginary line around the centre of the Earth. The areas around the equator are the parts of the planet closest to the Sun.

export Something that is sent from one country to be sold in another.

fertile Soil that will grow plenty of crops.

humid Warm and damp.

hurricane A storm with very strong winds.

independence A country ruled by another country gains independence when it begins ruling itself.

latitude Imaginary lines that run horizontally around the Earth.

longitude Imaginary lines that run vertically around the Earth.

map projection The process of forming a flat atlas map by 'stretching' a globe.

monsoon A strong South-Asian wind that usually also brings heavy rain.

northern hemisphere The half of the Earth north of the equator.

peninsula A narrow area of land that sticks out far into the sea.

permanent Something that will last.

population The people who live in a place or country.

southern hemisphere The half of the Earth south of the equator.

summit The highest point of a mountain.

tropical Very warm and humid conditions, as found in the areas around the equator.

volcanic Anything formed by a volcano.

Index

Editors: Karen Barker Smith
                        Stephanie Cole

Picture Research: Nicola Roe

Consultant: Penny Clarke

Photographic credits
Digital Stock/Corbis Corporation: 20, 25, 32, 35, 37, 41
John Foxx Images: 29, 31, 43, 45
Pictor International: 10, 17, 26, 51
Salariya Book Company: 15

Printed on paper from sustainable forests.

Printed and bound in Belgium.

Created, designed and produced by
The Salariya Book Company Ltd
Book House, 25 Marlborough Place,
Brighton BN1 1UB

Visit the Salariya Book Company at **www.salariya.com**

Published in Great Britain in 2002 by Hodder Wayland,
an imprint of Hodder Children's Books

A catalogue record for this book is available from the British Library.

ISBN 0 7502 3364 8

Hodder Children's Books, a division of Hodder Headline Limited
338 Euston Road, London NW1 3BH